TOGETHER
WE RISE

A Collection of Stories
From Women Who Came Together
During A Global Pandemic

*Exemplifying the Power of Women
Supporting Women*

THE LADY LEADERS BOOK CLUB

Foreword by
Lauren B. Jones & Leslie M. Vickrey

CONTENTS

FOREWORD

"Every woman's success should be an inspiration to another. We're strongest when we cheer each other on."
– Serena Williams

Our story as a collective began at an event to celebrate the launch of a book. Carefully planned down to the finest of details, we imagined this celebration would see us smiling for pictures, hugging it out, then going on with our lives without much fanfare.

That's not what happened.

Instead, we were forced to stay home with the rest of the world. A silver lining, though: The pandemic became the catalyst for inspiring events that have forever changed the lives of this group of women. What we decided to do *next*, in the face of adversity, is what makes this book so special.

We were all headed to an industry conference, and we wanted to carve out one special evening during our trip to celebrate a new author (Joyce Russell, who is part of this book collective) and the launch of her first book, *Put a Cherry on Top: Generosity in Life & Leadership*. We had a private dinner planned—what would've been a beautiful evening. We all knew each other; some on a very surface level, while deeper friendships had formed years ago for others. In that moment, we were simply coming together to support a fellow female leader. And that's what we find so impactful, as it's not something groups of women do often enough. Our hope is that, after reading this book, all women will do it more.

Everyone was confirmed. Tickets were booked, hotel reservations made, registrations complete. Then, the world shut down. We still wanted to celebrate our fellow female author, so we decided to organize a Zoom call. The rest of the world had quickly conformed to Zoom—why couldn't we?

We sent out all the virtual invitations and brought our group together. And on that first call, something special happened. We were lucky enough to have an author give us a first-hand account of her book. Joyce shared personal details regarding what inspired her to write specific chapters or anecdotes, and after that an idea was posed to the group, "Would you ladies have any interest in getting together regularly for a monthly book club?" We all adamantly said yes.

Thus, *The Lady Leaders Book Club* was born.

We quickly organized a regular book club and planned what we thought should come next. We read *How Women Rise* by Sally Helgesen and Marshall Goldsmith, then had one of our lady leaders present to the group on key takeaways and most inspired segments. The monthly meetings were meaningful, and they quickly became the highlight of our work-from-home lives.

Soon, we started pitching The Lady Leaders Book Club to more female authors (Dr. Stefanie Johnson, Erica Keswin, Heather Monahan and Gay Gaddis—to name a few). We began breaking our reading up with fun at-home Zoom events like a virtual cooking class, yoga, strength training, styling sessions, and more. We also started working together to tackle industry issues we felt passionately about. Born was the Diversity, Equity, and Inclusion group—an even larger group of women determined to solve pressing issues of inequality, representation, and beyond.

Keep in mind, the pandemic was still wreaking havoc on the world at that time. Some of our lady leaders had been laid off, started new roles, or were opening their own businesses. Then the true magic happened—we decided to work to support one another in every capacity. Women within the group began buying from one another, supporting each other's businesses, featuring their businesses on podcasts, referring each other for bigger roles, and making each other visible online. Perhaps most importantly, we started a movement to define our mission: #riseup.

With The Lady Leaders Book Club, a small group of women came together and found strength, devotion, acceptance, and true friendship—all of which inspired this book. We learned more about each other over the course of the past two years than we ever would have during one dinner. In this book are stories of women who have worked and strived to be the best in their field. Every story has its own trials, tribulations, and lessons to be shared. We hope that everyone reading this book will walk away feeling a connection, seeing themselves in a story, and knowing that you are *never* alone.

When you see a fellow female, reach out your hand to lend her support. Help her rise. Cheer her on. Together, we can destroy oppressive stereotypes and show the world we've got each other's backs. One lady leader at a time.

Lauren B. Jones & Leslie M. Vickrey

DREAM BIG – HOW TO SET GOALS, PRIORITIZE, AND ACHIEVE YOUR ASPIRATIONS

Joanie Bily

It was New Year's Eve, and I sat quietly by myself after putting my kids down to sleep. This would normally be a fun night out or maybe a romantic dinner with a good bottle of wine while we watched the ball drop, but not this year. It was a quiet night, which I spent thinking and reflecting on the past year and my plans for the future. It was normally an enjoyable time of self-reflection and planning for the new year. In the past, I've always enjoyed settings goals and having a few New Year's resolutions. This year was different.

I had just moved back to Long Island to be close to my parents and sisters after separating from my husband. My son, Chase, was about six at the time. My daughter, Ashley, was three. The kids and I moved into our new home right before Christmas, but I was lacking in Christmas spirit. I managed to get a Christmas tree up and decorated, and we celebrated with my parents and sisters. Overall, the holidays were a bit of a blur. I knew I was headed towards divorce and that my husband was moving more than halfway across the country. I also knew being a single working mom would bring a whole new set of challenges, especially with a career that required travel. I'd worked hard and put in the extra effort to build a successful career, but now I was faced with a new ultimatum—dealing with things on my own. I was overwhelmed with the thought of being there for my children. I wanted to be a hands-on mom and still maintain the career I had worked so hard for. I began doubting my decisions, feeling guilty for failing

1

to give my kids the upbringing I had envisioned. The truth is, I could feel myself teetering toward depression and a slump of self-disappointment. It was a very difficult point in my life, but it was also a turning point.

As a child, I dreamt of a happy and successful life. I wanted the perfect marriage, two kids, a house with the white picket fence, a great career, and the chance to travel and see the world. I was an ambitious dreamer. And while life didn't exactly go the way I'd dreamed or planned, I did achieve much of what I'd set my sights on. I am very fortunate and blessed to have two wonderful and loving children, an amazing family, and a rewarding career. I've had the chance to travel to many incredible places. I've had my share of successes and failures in life, but I always try to live life to the fullest. I credit my successes and accomplishments to three main things:

1) Confidence, which my parents instilled in me at a young age. I've always believed I could accomplish anything I set my mind to;

2) Goal setting—if you want to achieve your dreams, you need to set goals, then plan and pursue them relentlessly; and

3) Work ethic. You must be willing to put in the effort, hard work, and dedication to make things happen.

When you are not bound by limitations, you will dream bigger.

I specifically remember my mother telling me, "If you want to be the President of the United States, you can be." She made me realize I was in charge of my life. No one could hold me back.

My sisters and I were consistently reminded of our potential. We were told to work hard for what we wanted to achieve in life. I recognize not everyone is lucky enough to be raised with that support and encouragement. We all have different upbringings and family dynamics, and there is no perfect formula for creating confidence. My parents instilled love, confidence, and the importance of work ethic in all of us. I now see it was my upbringing that propelled me to push forward and keep reaching for the stars, especially as a woman. If I could go back and talk to my younger self, I would tell her to dream bigger and go for it. I now believe that I could have, and should have, dreamed bigger. Sure, my childhood dreams might have seemed big enough, but now I know there is no such thing as "a dream too big."

What is Dreaming Big?

What does it mean to dream big? Ask five people and each will likely offer a different definition. For me, dreaming big means capturing the desire to believe you can create, experience, or achieve something new. This dream involves something that will truly make you happy and fulfilled. Dreaming big creates an inner drive to push yourself, discover yourself, and grow as you reach a specific goal or objective. Your dream keeps you focused and determined on your path to accomplishing personal and professional goals.

Consider these questions as you decide how big you want to dream:

- How can you discover your abilities and grow as a person unless you're willing to step in a new direction?
- How can you make yourself stand out in a crowd when you place limitations on yourself?
- How much regret will you have if you know you could have pursued bigger dreams, but chose not to?

When you are not bound by limitations, you will dream bigger. You'll know that you can do better than you are doing now, and that there is much more for you to accomplish.

Setting Goals to Achieve Your Dreams

Best-selling author Tony Robbins puts it this way, "Setting goals is the first step in turning the invisible into the visible." As I mentioned before, I've always loved setting goals. Anyone who has ever worked for me would tell you that. Goals are excellent for mapping out specific objectives you wish to achieve. These could include saving money, losing weight, going back to college to complete your degree, running a marathon, getting a new job or promotion, or buying a car or house. One of the most important aspects of goal setting is tuning into your intuitive compass of wants and desires. This way, you'll set goals that are important to *you*. You set the course, and you own the path to achieve your goal.

Years ago, I started a practice of working with my employees to set personal and professional goals. This was something I had done for myself every year, and it helped me greatly. I instructed my employees to go through a simple exercise of five goal-setting steps:

1. Spend quality time thinking about what you want to accomplish this year.
2. Take time to write down your goals and aspirations.
3. Be specific about steps/actions you will take to achieve them.
4. Keep the list in a safe, but visible place (I always suggest having a copy in your wallet).
5. Revisit your goals on a regular basis to track progress and stay on course.

I would never ask my employees to share their personal goals because I believe those should remain private, but I did ask them to share their professional goals. By sharing them with me, I could understand what they wanted to achieve and support them in doing so.

One day, I was visiting one of my teams in Tampa, Florida, and I could see that a young man who had worked for me for two years was anxious to speak with me.

"Joanie, I have to tell you something," he said with joy in his voice. "Last year, you helped me with goal setting. I was living in an apartment, barely making ends meet." Obviously, I knew he had been successful at work over the last year and was consistently a strong performer. He went on to tell me that he was making more money than he had ever made, he'd saved enough to buy his first home, and he was about to buy a ring and propose to his girlfriend. He then opened his wallet and pulled out a piece of paper with his handwritten goals. The paper was worn around the edges, and you could tell it had been referred to many times. "Look at my goals," he said excitedly. I can't remember exactly what those black-inked words said, but it was something like this:

1. *Pay off credit card debt*
2. *Earn 100K*
3. *Buy my first house*
4. *Get engaged*

He proudly declared that he was on track to achieve each goal. He thanked me, and he was so heartfelt in telling me that his goals wouldn't have materialized unless he had taken the time to plan and write out what he wanted to accomplish, and then keep his goals in his wallet so he could continue working towards them. He was a true testament to the power of the approach. I was absolutely thrilled that he embraced the process and was achieving his goals.

The Foundational Fs

As years went by, I refined my goal-setting process for work and personal objectives. I would set goals around work promotions, sales achievements, buying a new home or car, exercise, savings, travel, vacations, family time, etc. I was always ambitious when it came to growing my career. At the same time, it was extremely important for me to focus on my family. I followed a simple approach towards setting and achieving personal goals which I refer to as the *Foundational Fs*: Faith, Family & Friends, Finance, Fitness, and FUN. Each F represents an important part of your life, and setting goals related to the Foundational Fs can help you achieve your best life.

Faith: Whether you are religious or spiritual is a personal preference. I think of faith as having dimensions beyond religion or spirituality. Faith is related to positive change that you and others can bring to your life. If you are religious, faith could involve regular worship; if you are spiritual, you might have a regular meditation practice or like to spend time in nature. The faith component of achieving dreams can involve anything positive that helps you be your best self and achieve your big dreams. Faith provides a basis for setting personal goals that will facilitate your personal growth.

Family & Friends: The goals you specify in this aspect of your life can strengthen or build your relationships. Whether you establish these goals to benefit your relationship with your significant other, spouse, children, siblings, parents, friends, or other relationships, they all require your time and attention. Your goals regarding family could involve helping them cope with a difficult time, communicating with them more, or facilitating changes to solve problems. This aspect includes all you want to achieve for your family and friends.

Finance: Keeping your finances in order is a vital factor of success. That doesn't mean you must be wealthy, but you need enough to cover your expenses, save for the future, and enjoy vacations and other forms of entertainment. Your financial objectives should include all your personal and business objectives, such as investing in businesses or properties, buying your first home or retirement home, saving, and creating a career that will maximize your earnings. It's impossible to concentrate on something else in life when you are constantly worrying about finances and debts. Creating a financially stable life brings stability and alleviates stress.

Fitness: Improving your health and fitness will help you achieve your goals in other aspects of life. Without good health and fitness, you can't give 100 percent. Wealth and success mean nothing without good health. Doing everything possible to attain and enjoy your peak fitness level makes things more exciting. There are very few people with perfect health records, and for most, certain health problems cannot be entirely resolved regardless of how hard we work. It certainly doesn't mean we can't try to be at our best. We must set fitness goals that can help us work towards our best selves. Self-care is vital to our goals and the fulfillment of our lives.

Fun: This aspect of life is just as important as all the others. It's too easy to neglect fun while building a career. Fun includes all the things that make you happy, bring you joy, and fulfill your purpose. Fun is the final aspect that ties together all the other Fs, and I would call it the most essential of the Fs. It's much easier to achieve if the first four Fs are already in order. There's no doubt in my mind that you and I were made to find, make, and enjoy as much fun as possible.

Taking Care of Yourself

On that pivotal New Year's Eve, I thought of all the people I've helped with goal setting, and I suddenly realized I needed to take more of my own advice.

I decided to spend quality time writing down a statement detailing what I wanted to achieve and improve in each area. I needed to reevaluate where I was in life and what I wanted to focus on. I wrote out specific "F" goals: Family—ensure I have the proper care and attention for my children while I'm working. Find a wonderful nanny to help take care of them; Faith—we would attend Church on Sundays together; Finance —I would save a certain amount each month for my children's education; Fitness—we will eat balanced, healthy meals, and I will keep exercising four times a week; Fun—I would plan a vacation to take the kids to Disney World, just the three of us. It may sound simple, but I had to get the basics in place and focus on my priorities.

After I'd set my goals, I typed them up and printed three copies. I kept one in my wallet so I could always have them with me. I put the second copy on the inside of my closet door, so I could see them while I was getting dressed in the morning. I put the third copy in my journal, which I kept in my nightstand, so I could pray about them each night or morning and set my intentions for working towards my goals that day. I always kept those goals with me, and I am proud to say I achieved them.

I'd always heard that when you set goals you need to make them specific, measurable, attainable, and you must write them down and keep them visible. You might still get off track at times even if you do all that, but you can always adjust your goals as necessary. And there's no law that says you must check every box and achieve each goal perfectly every year. It might take years to achieve a goal. The idea is to keep your goals visible and keep working towards self-improvement. Doing so will help you stay focused on what is truly important to you.

I'd always wanted to run the New York City marathon, which was one of my fitness goals for many years. Sometimes, I laughed at myself for writing it down, but deep inside it was something I knew I wanted to achieve. Some years, there were reasons why I couldn't commit to it. Being a single mom with two young children and working full time doesn't give you a lot of free time to train for a marathon. Still, I kept it on the list, and eventually when my kids were older, I decided to go for it.

Running the NYC marathon was one of the best days of my life. I was fortunate to have family and friends come out to support me, and I enjoyed every step along the way. I loved seeing all the spectators lining the streets and cheering us runners on. It was a day I'll never forget, and I am so grateful that I made that commitment. I learned that if you want something bad enough and are willing to put in the effort, you can accomplish anything. I also learned to truly enjoy the experience. I don't just mean the final race—I had to enjoy the journey that came before achieving the goal. I enjoyed planning my runs, running for longer on weekends, and logging and tracking my progress. The entire experience was wonderful.

If you're like me, it can be easy to take life too seriously. Setting goals and achieving them can become grim and mechanical. Accomplishing objectives is much easier for me when I love what I'm doing. Many objectives aren't achieved because they aren't perceived as enjoyable—they're more like obligations. I credit a big part of my career success to the fact that I absolutely love what I do. It's easier to put in the effort and planning when you're dedicated and enjoy what you do.

When it comes to achieving goals, endurance is required. It's not just about building up physical endurance, it's about creating the mental toughness to overcome adversity and keep going. Webster's dictionary defines endurance as:

1. the ability to withstand hardship or adversity, *especially*: the ability to sustain a prolonged stressful effort or activity (ex: a marathon runner's *endurance)*
2. the act or an instance of enduring or suffering (ex: *endurance* of many hardships)
3. PERMANENCE, DURATION (ex: the *endurance* of the play's importance)

I find the definition of endurance sums up what it takes to achieve your personal and professional goals. Life is full of obstacles and hurdles that we must overcome. We all face adversity and challenges daily, and we need to find ways to manage. Life is not perfect—mine is certainly far from it. I needed to overcome adversity and find a way to create the life I wanted. That took endurance, mental toughness, grit, and confidence. I have experienced other hardships and obstacles over the years, and having goals and a plan has always helped me move forward. Obstacles will never stop me from striving to do better, personally improving, living my best life, and doing the best job I can as a mom, daughter, friend, spouse, employee, boss, and Christian.

Is It Possible to Have It All?

Setting goals has helped me achieve many personal and professional successes. It has helped me organize my priorities and focus on important initiatives that I needed and wanted to do. I admit there are times I hold everything together with duct tape and rubber bands, but I still get it done. I also make time for myself to exercise, read, write, pray, and hang out with friends and family.

Trying to juggle a family and a career is a challenge for anyone. It's important to spend time identifying your top priorities and goals for your family *and* your career. Be realistic and specific about what is required and what you want to accomplish. Be clear about what you can and cannot do. Avoid taking on too much—otherwise you may set yourself up for failure. You might realize you need help or that you should start saying "no" to certain things. Be reasonable and certain about what you can and cannot handle.

A few years ago, I began a new goal-setting practice that might be even more impactful. I reflected and wrote down all I was proud of accomplishing each year. The first year I did it, I ended up with a few pages of reflections. It forced me to take a moment and appreciate myself. As a busy working mom, it's rare to pat yourself on the back and appreciate all you do for everyone else. Recognizing all the positive contributions I'd made over the past year was a meaningful exercise. I encourage everyone to do it. *Especially* women.

Over ten years have passed since that difficult New Year's Eve. I will never forget that turning point in my life. I am grateful for the incredible support and guidance I have received from my family, friends, and mentors. I am especially thankful for the practice of reflecting on my accomplishments and setting aspirations, intentions, and goals for the new year.

I hope my story encourages you to focus on dreaming big, prioritizing what's important, and achieving personal and professional success. Search your soul for inspiration. Dig deep and push to understand what is most important to you. Most of all, believe in yourself. You can accomplish amazing things. Don't give up on your dreams for yourself, your family, or your career. As they say, life is a marathon, not a sprint. Make sure you build your endurance to keep yourself on track. And remember, it's never too late to DREAM BIG!

Joanie Bily

Joanie Bily is currently President of RemX Staffing, Chief Workforce Analyst at EmployBridge, and a Board Member and Officer at the American Staffing Association. She has spent over 25 years in the staffing and recruiting industry leading sales and operations, including executive roles with two of the largest employment firms in the world.

Throughout her career, Joan has led high-performing teams and world-class customer success programs. She has been named to Staffing Industry Analysts' Global Power 150 Women in Staffing list the last five consecutive years and was recognized with the World Staffing Summit Award as the No. 1 staffing professional to watch for in 2021. She is passionate about goal setting and helping others achieve their personal and professional ambitions. Her favorite role is as a proud mom to her two children, Chase and Ashley.

Joanie is often called upon as an employment executive and authority to provide commentary on the job market, careers, workplace trends, and to speak to the talent supply and demand cycles that impact U.S. employers. She is a regular keynote speaker at industry conferences and is a frequent contributor to the Fox Business Network. Her commentary on the employment market has been featured on media outlets like Fox and Fox Business Network, Bloomberg, Associated Press, CNBC, MSNBC, CNN, ABC, PBS, The Wall Street Journal, U.S. News & World Report, and Forbes.

https://www.linkedin.com/in/joanie-bily-b959712/
https://twitter.com/JoanieBily
www.joaniebily.com

WHAT IF KRYPTONITE ACTUALLY MADE SUPERMAN STRONGER?

Kelly Boykin

I used to look at successful people and marvel at their journeys. From afar, it looked effortless; they marched forward at a steady pace with no detours or obstacles. I assumed they led charmed lives—they knew some life hack that gave them clear confidence and direction. Of course, it was all an illusion. There are certainly those who experience pivotal events which change the direction of their career. But for me, it was simple. I've had the right person say or do the right thing at the right time, creating a series of well-placed motivations or course corrections when I needed them most. Maybe I was extremely lucky. But more likely, I was paying attention and was open to the nuggets of wisdom that were generously shared with me.

Let's back up a bit. When I was a little girl, I wanted to be a hero. I wanted superpowers. It was more than a wish, even—it felt imminent. I imagined myself with super strength or magical powers, and I knew it was just a matter of time until I discovered what they were. I would see how fast I could run or jump, hoping I would be able to fly. Inspired by reruns of *I Dream of Jeannie*, I'd fold my arms and blink to make my room clean itself. *Bewitched* was inspirational too, though I could never learn to wiggle my nose.

You probably weren't expecting me to say all that. This entire book about women overcoming real obstacles, and here I am talking about superheroes? It's okay, you're in the right place. Stay with me for a moment.

I realize admiring Superman isn't all that unusual. Being powerful and heroic is appealing, especially to children. So, I pictured myself as that hero—cape and all. I knew my powers would come. When I just got a *little* older. *Any* time now, they'll come!

Of course, they didn't. And I eventually realized they never would. I adapted to my mortal life with the false confidence that little kids have. I've always found it ironic how small children, who have contributed nothing to society aside from their incredible existence, often have more confidence than many grown adults who've accomplished so much in the world. Where does that confidence start? And where does it go?

I'm not sure when or why it changed for me. People saw me as a cheerful, strong, outspoken person who could do anything. Internally, I was very different. Like so many young girls, my self-confidence was shaky. And as I got older, that feeling didn't really go away. I thought everyone else was smarter, more talented, and prettier. I worried about what everyone thought of me and was devastated if someone didn't like me—not just my family or friends, total strangers, too. I've since matured, but elements of that person still exist. For example, unless a server openly spits on my food, I'm probably not going to send it back. To avoid them thinking I'm a diva, I will eat that bowl of mushy pasta with overcooked sauce. It's a mystery how I became this way. Is confidence a learned behavior, or was I missing a certain gene? Did the mean girls in middle school affect me more than I thought? Was it the realization that I was never going to be able to flip a car with one perfectly manicured finger? No idea. Somehow, I found myself with all this self-doubt and no superpowers to save me.

Throughout this book, you'll hear inspiring stories from my incredible friends, many of whom have conquered very real challenges in their lives. My biggest obstacle is currently, and has always been, me.

See, aren't you glad you're still reading?

Most of Our Confidence Issues are Not Based in Reality

Here's the thing—Growing up, I was well-liked and good at sports. I was smart and successful at almost everything I tried. I know so because *other* people told me. I couldn't really see it, though. Funny, if they'd told me I was a smartass or a train wreck, I would have believed them immediately. But compliments? Those I didn't believe.

There's a saying "don't believe your own press." It's a warning that reminds egomaniacs not to let praise from others go to their heads. I've never had this problem. In fact, it would have been better if I had believed even a bit of what was said about me. Later in life, this feeling was identified as what we now call Imposter Syndrome. My adolescent self would struggle to list my strengths, but I was keenly aware of my flaws:

- I was too sensitive, a people pleaser, and I cared too much what others thought of me.
- I was direct and often physically incapable of holding my tongue.
- I did things too quickly and made mistakes.
- I was easily distracted and daydreamed too often.
- I was disorganized.
- I had the worst sense of direction of any known mortal.

The list seemed long and insurmountable back then. But when I look at it through a different lens, I can see it's a list of my superpowers. Well, except for that last one, which has seen zero improvement during my lifetime (thank you, Google Maps)!

Candor and Constructive Feedback are Gifts

Let's fast forward a bit—I stumbled blindly into staffing. I knew nothing about the industry, just that it sounded like a cool gig. I was told I could make decent money, help people find jobs, and that there would never be a dull moment. Sold! But what do you do with a person who fears rejection and is obsessed with being liked? If you're sadistic and cruel, you put them in sales.

I was terrified. Sure, I can talk to anyone (my cat is a good listener), but cold calling was torture. Now, to some of you "cold calling" might mean emailing someone you don't know or picking up the phone and calling a stranger. 20 years ago, it meant physically driving to office buildings, walking past security like you belonged there, ignoring the *No Soliciting* signs on the door, and boldly asking for business. I can't tell you how many people yelled at me or how many buildings I was kicked out of (I've blocked those memories). I had no idea what I was doing, and I went home every night reliving the rejection and scorn that came with sales.

It suddenly seemed like my shiny new career was about to crash. But a generous peer completely changed my perspective with one simple statement: "No one is rejecting you personally, Kelly. In fact, they don't know you well enough to reject you. It's not about you, so just let it go." I listened to this well-timed advice, and doing so provided me tremendous freedom. When I depersonalized the rejection, the pressure faded. I was able to relax. And when I began to just be myself, something interesting happened. I discovered that my desire to be liked, my humor and candor, could be leveraged to create an immediate connection with people. They would want to help me. Whoa!

The People That Can Make You Better are Probably Already in Your Life

Most of us can point to someone who impacted our lives—a coach, teacher, or family member. For me it was our franchise owner, Mike. I admire much about him, and at the top of that list was his ability to make people shine. Mike's sincere desire to help was obvious, and it created a magical space of trust. He recognized strengths in me that I didn't see and pushed me to take advantage of them. He also provided me critical feedback in a way that never felt negative—it felt like a gift. I knew he was personally invested in my success. This was his universal leadership style, and he got the best out of everyone with it.

As a true ally, Mike removed barriers from my path and pushed me to step up. With each success, my confidence grew. He entrusted me with more of his organization, which deepened my loyalty. I was committed to growing his business. It was a powerful circle of success.

At a corporate function one year, we both watched in pain as other owners took the stage to accept awards. Annoyed, I looked at him and said, "You're going to be on that stage next year."

And he was. We worked hard, hired incredible people, and grew the business. I made great money that year, but the pride I felt when he won Franchisee of the Year was deeply personal to me. He eventually sold the business and retired, but 20 years later I'm still quoting him daily. I spoke to him recently and expressed my gratitude for everything he taught me. I was surprised when he responded, "Funny, I think I learned as much from you as you did from me."

I hope everyone has a Mike in their life. You probably do already, you just need to open your eyes and notice them. And if you don't immediately find your Mike, be a hero to someone else until you find your own. Investments in other people will reward you tenfold down the road.

Don't Wait for Your Heroes to Find You — Learn From Everyone Around You

I was becoming more comfortable with myself as a leader, but occasionally that old list would reappear in the form of someone shining a light on my flaws. People would say:

- "You can't be a great leader if you care what people think."
- "You are too collaborative, stop inviting others' opinions and make the decision yourself, otherwise you will undermine your authority."
- "You are too invested in other people's success."

These were valid points. I did need to be tough, decisive, and hold people accountable as a leader. But I was doing it *my way*.

I'm going to tell you something that you've probably heard many times before and likely ignored. You are awesome, and you already have superpowers. I don't know you, we haven't met, but trust me on this. Your strengths and weaknesses are not opposite things, they are closely related. Criminal tendencies aside, most flaws can also be strengths. Here is a real-life example:

I'm high energy. I make decisions quickly and get things done faster than average. It might be a small decision or a large one—like that time I decided to pick out and purchase a car during a 30-minute lunch break. These qualities are good but can also cause me to jump to a solution without considering all the options. On the flip side, I know a great guy who is one of the smartest and most thorough people I know. He's analytical, detail-oriented, and rarely makes a mistake. The downside is he can overthink and drag out decisions, even very simple ones like which beer to order. His decisive, fast-paced wife is usually halfway through her beer before he places an order. Like my lack of direction, we may never solve the beer thing.

Somewhere along the way, I stopped focusing on overcoming my flaws and learned to unleash them as powerful weapons. From that long list of weaknesses also comes candor, creative problem solving, and the ability to use humor to put others at ease and foster mutual trust. I can deliver tough feedback in a way that is heard—because it comes from a place of sincerity. People know I'm not just interested in their success—I'm committed to it. There are qualities on your list that you could morph into a strength.

As I said, the right person and some well-timed advice helped shape my path. I've spent years being a sponge and learning from those around me, and it's been extremely rewarding when I can pay that gift forward. I'm sure I have failed in this plenty of times, but it's important that I help others see that they already have the superpowers they need to be successful. If they gain meaningful guidance from me today that makes a difference in their lives, perhaps they will quote me in 20 years and help the next group rise up.

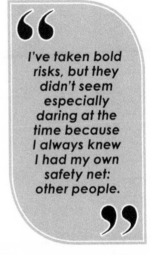

I've taken bold risks, but they didn't seem especially daring at the time because I always knew I had my own safety net: other people.

I'm fortunate to know some remarkable leaders whom I admire and who value me. The best of them have pushed me to take risks. They enabled me to do big things, and I trusted them to have my back. These days, my career has evolved. I find myself less reliant on guidance and protection from others.

I recently discovered a fitting analogy. Picture a trapeze artist somersaulting and flying 50 feet in the air. We marvel at their skill. While what they are doing seems death defying, we notice there is a safety net underneath them. With fear removed from the equation, they are free to be creative and brave as they amaze us with their incredible feats. But what if they noticed that the net was gone, and it had been for a long time? They would realize they didn't have the safety and security they assumed was there—they had been doing it themselves all along.

I'll never possess the bravery or remote athletic ability of a trapeze artist. Nevertheless, I've stretched and flexed, I've leaped forward and reinvented myself. I've taken bold risks, but they didn't seem especially daring at the time because I always knew I had my own safety net: other people.

Like our trapeze artist, my net has been gone for a long time now, and I've been thriving under my own powers. After an entire lifetime of wishing for superpowers, I finally realized I could fly all along.

Kelly Boykin

Kelly is the Senior Vice President of Global Alliances. She manages partnership strategy with the world's best and largest Managed Services Providers around the world.

She is a 25-year veteran of the staffing industry who began her career leading sales and recruiting teams across North America, all while working with top Fortune 500 brands.

Kelly is active in the staffing industry, including the American Staffing Association (ASA) and Staffing Industry Analysts (SIA). She is particularly passionate about supporting women in the industry. Kelly is the Chair of the Women in Leadership Council for the American Staffing Association, and she mentor's women in staffing through the ASA Mentoring Program. She has been recognized for the past three years by Staffing Industry Analysts on the Global Power 150 Most Influential Women in Staffing list.

https://www.linkedin.com/in/kellyboykin/

THE REWARDS OF RISK TAKING

Sue Burnett

I never thought of myself as a risk-taker, but I truly was. Growing up in a small town in Arkansas, the only working women I knew were schoolteachers. I was determined not to be a housewife like my mother was. I wanted a career, but I never dreamed how big that career would be! My career journey spans over 50 years, in which time I've taken many risks both personally and professionally.

After graduating with a degree in journalism from the University of Arkansas in 1968, I got a job at a TV station in Little Rock as a typist making $2.00 an hour—minimum wage at the time. After six months, I was promoted to Assistant Promotion Director and given a raise to $375 a month. Then, I saw an ad in the newspaper for a job paying $500 a month for someone with a journalism degree. The person had to be willing to travel, and I was, so I applied for the job and was interviewed.

One day at the TV station, I was typing the daily log while my boss read the paper with his feet up on his desk beside me. He told me to go get him a cup of coffee. I asked him to please get it himself, as I was far too busy. When I came into work the next day, the Operations Manager told me I was being fired because I had refused to get coffee for my boss. I was shocked!

The next day, I got a call from the company I'd interviewed with and was offered the job for $500 monthly. That led to a great adventure working for the nation's largest dairy co-op, where I would be writing speeches and planning conventions. Two weeks before the national convention, I got a phone call from one of my sorority sisters asking whether I wanted to come and live in Houston with her sister-in-law, who had just graduated from college. Without thinking it over, I said yes and gave my two weeks' notice. I drove to Houston the day after we got back from the convention. At 24, I was moving to a city where I didn't know anyone, didn't have a job, didn't know my roommate or where I would be living, and had $500 in savings. That was the first of my big risks.

Luckily, my new roommate turned out to be great. I went to three employment agencies for help finding a job. One of the services offered me a job as a personnel consultant on straight commission. I called my father and asked for his advice. He told me that if it didn't work out, at least I would know where the jobs were. That was how I embarked upon my career in personnel consulting—my second big risk.

I quickly discovered I loved helping people find jobs, and that I had a real knack for it. Six months into this new adventure, my manager resigned to be a stay-at-home mother. They promoted me to manager at the age of 24, and I was suddenly overseeing recruiters who had been there much longer than me. The agency did well under my leadership, and I was making $2,000 a month. I was single and dated freely since I was not interested in getting married. One of the people I dated was Rusty Burnett, a divorcee with two children. I never considered marrying Rusty—until he proposed to me! I heard myself say yes without thinking. That was my third big risk.

On our honeymoon, Rusty suggested I start my own personnel agency. I was only 27, and I had no ambition to own a company. We also didn't have the money to start a new company because Rusty had entered our marriage with debt and had monthly child support and alimony to pay. Five months after we got married, my boss was not paying the bills for our company due to his divorce. Rusty told me it was time to go out on my own. So, seven months after we'd married, I quit my job and started my own company—my fourth big risk.

We went to a bank and used my car as collateral to borrow $10,000. In 1974, women could not get bank loans without having their husband sign for them. I hired five people and rented office space. After one year, we were profitable and able to repay the loan. Two years after I'd started the agency, Rusty decided to quit his job and join me at the company. He didn't know anything about recruiting, and I was too busy to teach him. Our parents thought we were crazy having Rusty quit a job with stability and excellent benefits at a large oil company, but we took the risk anyway—my fifth big risk.

During a five-year period of my twenties, I took the biggest risks of my life. Many of these decisions were made quickly and without much deliberation. Sometimes, weighing the pros and cons too intensely keeps you from taking a leap of faith that can really pay off.

Many people have told me they could never have worked with their spouse. Fortunately, we were excellent business partners. Rusty became a good recruiter and was skilled in accounting and database programming. He introduced computers to our company. His strengths were my weaknesses. My strengths were interacting with clients, training our staff, promoting the company, and being a top recruiter. We worked together for 40 years, and he's always been the wind beneath my wings and my biggest motivator and supporter.

Finding What Works for You

In the beginning, our company consisted mostly of permanent placement recruiters. By the late 1970s, we decided to open a temporary staffing division. It became very successful. The revenue from that division exceeded our direct placement revenue. We also opened an office in Austin and multiple locations in Houston. We acquired a staffing company in El Paso in 1996 and another with offices in Dallas and San Antonio in 2001. Those were risks that paid off.

Other risks we took weren't as successful. We tried franchising in the early 1990s. The Gulf War broke out the month both of our new franchises opened, and we were forced to sell them off. That taught me that I did not want to be a franchisor—I wanted to keep all our offices company-owned and in Texas.

In 1997, we were offered the opportunity to be a part of a roll up of other personnel companies and go public. I was reluctant, but Rusty was very excited. Fate intervened—in August of 1997, three months after we'd signed the papers, the stock market crashed. No companies could go public with IPOs for at least three months after that. Our agreement was written so that if we could not go public within 30 days of the go-public date, the agreement would be void. I was relieved we did not have to be a part of a public company.

In all the years we've been running our company, there have been many recessions and a once-in-a-lifetime pandemic. Through all the ups and downs, our revenue has fluctuated by millions. After the 2009 recession, I received a call from a friend who was a business broker. His client was an international staffing company that was looking to buy a company in the United States. I wasn't interested in selling the company, but I agreed to meet with them. They made us an incredible offer that Rusty felt we couldn't turn down. The company told me they would keep me on as President for a year after the sale. After that, my career would be over. But I wasn't ready to retire, and the prospect of it caused me to spiral into a depression. We turned the offer down.

A few months later, the same broker friend called to tell me he'd heard about a woman in Missouri who had a large staffing company that had just established an ESOP (Employee Stock Ownership Program). I didn't know what an ESOP was, so I called this woman in October after her company had just closed the deal. She gave me the number of the company that had helped put their ESOP together. The manager flew out to meet us in November of 2010, and I told Rusty I felt that transitioning to employee ownership was our company's future.

Unfortunately, we couldn't ask any companies in our industry for information about running successful ESOPs, because they are rare in the staffing industry. We were taking a big gamble.

The ESOP team that had helped the Missouri company met with us on December 1st, and we told them our fiscal year ended on Christmas Eve. They said it would take 60 to 90 days to complete all the requirements necessary to convert to an ESOP. We told them they had 24 days to do it, and they said I had to tell my staff the next day. We got all of our out-of-town offices on a conference call and gathered our 80 Houston employees into our largest conference room. I told them Rusty and I had decided to give our stock in the company to them as a gift, at no cost to them personally. There was silence in the room; everyone looked puzzled. We continued to explain how it would all work, but it was such a new concept that they couldn't understand it.

Luckily, we had luncheons planned with each office for Christmas. During each of these lunches, I explained that this stock would translate to money for their retirement in addition to the 401(k) plan we already had. Some of our staff started to understand what this could mean for them.

It ended up taking three years before the staff genuinely understood what it meant, as our stock price increased each year and they saw the monetary value of their stock holdings increase along with it. "Think like an owner" became our slogan. Much of our staff took it to heart. Unfortunately, most of our staffing employees don't understand the employee ownership concept, so it has been a constant education process for them.

We didn't want the company to take any risks or borrow money to pay me and Rusty off (to complete the ESOP). We decided we would be paid out of the profits of the company, which would take at least seven years. It was another big risk—we didn't know what the future economy would be like. For me, it was great because I could continue to run the company, and everything would remain the same. No one would lose their jobs, which often happens when companies are bought by other staffing companies.

Since I was approaching 65 and Rusty was turning 70 at the time, many of our managers asked us about our succession plan. The ESOP was the answer. We could transfer ownership of our stock to our staff and to our long-term temporary staffing employees, who worked toward a vesting goal. The value of the company was set by an appraisal firm. Since we'd just received a legitimate offer for our company a few months prior, the value of the company was set at that price. As an ESOP, the company does not pay taxes, so Rusty and I could be paid out of the profits. Fortunately, our company did well during the next seven years, and we were paid off in six and a half years. ESOP trustees have told me it's very unusual for an ESOP to be paid off early.

> **Today, I know what my legacy will be and I'm happy to share my success with those who made my achievements possible.**

Now our ESOP is 11 years old, and it has been very successful. We've seen a 160% increase in our stock value, and our staff is excited about the stock price announcement each year. I have a monthly video call with the entire staff each month where we announce our financials and profits. This way, we're transparent and inclusive with them as owners of the company.

We set our core values a few years ago with the help of our employee owners. "We own it" was the first value. Our company's culture is family first, and our staff is 95% women. I believe in the Golden Rule: treat everyone like family. This has resulted in most of our staff being very long tenured, with many having spent over 10, 20, 30, or even 40 years with the company. The ESOP has motivated our managers and staff to stay with us as their stock grows.

Our culture of employee ownership was critical when the COVID-19 pandemic struck in 2020. It was a challenging time in our history, comparable only to the oil crash of 1986 (when the plummeting price of oil sent unemployment in Houston skyrocketing to 12%). The pandemic was the first time since then where the company had lost money three months in a row. We had never had a time where companies were literally shut down for two months or longer. I knew there had to be layoffs and cost cutbacks. Our management team had an owner mentality about the situation, and they made many painful, but necessary decisions to cut staff. Many of our staff members volunteered to take salary cuts. I explained to our employee owners that we wanted to protect the value of our stock, which they understood. By cutting costs, we ended up being profitable in 2020. In 2021, we had a record year.

Taking risks has been vital to my success. I took a chance being in the staffing business in 1970, and I ended up owning my own staffing firm. Forty years later, we took a chance on employee ownership and turned hundreds of other people into owners of a staffing firm. I've always believed that if you don't gamble, you can't win. And my attitude has always been that if something doesn't work out, I'll simply do something else.

Too many people are risk-averse. They settle for less than what they could have. Today, I know what my legacy will be. I'm happy to share my success with those who made my achievements possible. The ESOP money will truly change the lives of our employee owners. That's exciting!

Taking all those risks paid off. My life has genuinely exceeded my dreams! I look forward to what the future holds for the company and my life.

Sue Burnett

Sue Burnett is the founder and president of Burnett Specialists (Houston, Austin, El Paso, and San Antonio), and Choice Specialists (Dallas). Her 47-year-old company is ranked as the 16th largest employee-owned U.S. Firm by NCEO, the 10th top woman-owned business by DiversityBusiness.com, and the largest placement and 3rd largest staffing firm by the Houston Business Journal. Burnett Specialists was named one of the Top 100 Recruitment firms in the U.S. by Forbes Magazine.

Sue's honors include: Texas Businesswoman of the Year, Ernst & Young's Entrepreneur of the Year, NAWBO's Woman Business Owner of the Year, WBEA's Business Entrepreneur of the Year, Houston Business Journal's Most Admired CEO, Most Powerful Woman Award by the National Diversity Council, Staffing Industry's Top 100, Women's Enterprise's Woman of Excellence, and the Jr. Achievement's Legacy Award.

The University of Arkansas named Sue a Distinguished Alum and a Tower of Old Main, and she was inducted into the Journalism Hall of Fame. Sue and her husband, Rusty, were donors for the Sue Walk Burnett Journalism and Media Center at the University of Arkansas.

Sue serves on the Board of Directors of Junior Achievement, Better Business Bureau, and Goodwill Industries. She was the founder of the Best Places to Work awards in Houston, Austin, Dallas, & San Antonio.

https://www.linkedin.com/in/sue-burnett-44418a1/
Sue@burnettspecialists.com

LEAVE 'EM BETTER THAN YOU FOUND 'EM

Kendra Cato

My Tribe

A few years ago, I tried on a gorgeous, oh so soft, incredibly marked down camel wool coat and immediately felt like a powerhouse. It was on its way home with me before I remembered my first Chicago snowfall back when I was barely 20 years old. There I was, visiting for the first time and walking with my chin up like I belonged (just as my father taught me), in a camel thrift store dress coat and a pair of cowboy boots that my mama, Red, snagged on clearance because she knew I'd love them.

Thinking of the young girl who fell in love with State Street that day made me smile. The girl who, without even realizing, changed the course of her entire life with a single decision: to make Chicago her home. I shook my head and chuckled at her fearlessness—she'd packed up her things in small town Ohio and waved goodbye to the only world she'd ever known.

Weeks later, I walked into a women-in-tech event hosted by an incredible female leader whom I greatly admired. I wore my new coat and prayed it would help disguise my Imposter Syndrome. Every woman who walked on stage was given a glowing intro. These powerful women gripped the mic with a smile and shared their stories, and they all expressed immense gratitude for their tribe.

I thought about the women in my life who'd lifted me up, made me feel welcome, and invited me to share such moments in this city I call home. Some of them were my closest friends, while others had no idea the things I'd been through or the times I hadn't felt worthy. Still, they all managed to be there for me when I needed it most.

Then, a woman with a soothing voice and a mind-boggling success story took the stage and captivated the crowd. During her closing statement, she mentioned that despite everything she had been through, the *only* thing she wished she'd done differently was be kinder to her mother.

I blinked away tears as I thought of how Red had grown up in a home with very little kindness, yet she'd never sent me to bed without saying she loved me. This shy young woman would always smile when strangers expressed their surprise after she'd answered, "Yes, this is my daughter." A woman who painstakingly drew fairytale books with princesses that looked like me and who kept a Black angel atop the Christmas tree every year.

It wasn't until I was putting on my new coat to leave that it struck me—that last speaker's distinctly beautiful voice had sounded just like my late grandmother's. How had I missed it?

My mind cleared as the scent of my Grandma Bea's sweet sandalwood perfume overcame me, and in my mind, I heard her say, "I'm so proud of you, honey." Tears welled in my eyes yet again, but this time I was smiling as I slowly bundled up to leave. The cold air felt light when I got outside. I decided to walk a bit before catching a cab.

As I walked—through a snowy silence you only experience when you've lived in a city long enough to recognize it—it struck me that all my missteps, and my big steps into the unknown, were the most important moments that had shaped me and my future.

The Missteps (and Big Steps) That Make Us

My first misstep upon arriving to Chicago? A brief stint with a public relations firm. It took a few months for me to realize it wasn't for me. I've always had a business mind, and I'd flirted with the idea of getting an MBA. But as my father used to say to me, "Do you have MBA money?" So, I quickly decided to get into business writing instead.

My first big step into the unknown? Taking a cold-calling gig for a boutique mergers and acquisitions firm. They gave me a script and a phone, and I smiled, dialed, and quietly learned more about the analyst team on the other side of the building. They were responsible for the valuation services the firm provided. I began to think, "Maybe I can make my way over there..."

I stayed at that job and stepped outside of my comfort zone by striking up watercooler and bathroom convos with anyone I didn't recognize from the sales floor. It took several months and many $1 frozen dinners before I landed an interview for an editor role. I got the job, and I loved it. This was before social media, so our C-suite clients and private equity contacts never realized they were answering to a young Black girl fresh out of college.

I soon met someone and fell in love. So, when our parent company shut us down and I was forced to work a temp job, life was still good.

My next big step into the unknown was convincing a few folks from our team to launch a boutique mergers and acquisitions firm with a household name in the industry (now *that's* a good story). A couple years later, we hosted a holiday bash with nearly 70 employees and were doing well enough that I was able to quit working full-time to study my passion—interior design.

I was married two years later, and the real estate market was tanking. My husband and I decided to move to Oxford, UK. I was thrilled to be living abroad, but our savings were dwindling. I applied to any job I could find. After wrapping up a second interview with a high-end furniture designer at Chicago's Merchandise Mart, I was asked to fly home for the third and final interview. My husband and I agreed I should go despite the fact we'd be living apart for several months.

I prepared for that interview like my life depended on it. At first, everything was going great. But the last interview of the day with the head of HR felt … off. We were in person, so there was nothing to hide the fact that I was a young Black woman. I saw his jaw tense up the moment I walked into his office. It took me years to accept that there was nothing I could've done to change his mind.

And so, there I was with a misstep that left me with no design job or prospects during a global financial crisis and a husband 3,895 miles away. It took weeks for me to get out of bed and consider my exec-level client management experience and know-how to manage books.

I finally landed an interview with a tiny corporate law firm for a glorified office assistant role, and I convinced the partner to give me six months to prove my worth with the promise to renegotiate my pay.

It worked. I landed a better salary (still less than half of what I'd been making four years prior) and stayed on for a couple years while also taking on small design gigs. Eventually, the partner had me managing his key clients. The market began to recover, but my marriage was crumbling. I was soon focusing more on the partner's book of clients—a few of which were tech start-ups—and less on my own design business.

I began asking questions after seeing some of the checks these PE firms were cutting for a kid even younger than me to take an idea from the back of a napkin to market. It didn't take long for me to realize that banking and corporate law were quickly becoming prehistoric in the land of innovation. The software contracts I reviewed were foreign compared to our brick-and-mortar clients, but their growth—which I was witnessing firsthand—had my attention.

Suddenly, my father fell mysteriously ill. He died six months later. It has been ten years, and I'm still unable to express how hard his death was for all of us. This was a man of God who led our family and his congregation with his actions (though he was never short on words). He was a businessman who made Red blush by singing her love songs during our long rides home from church, who carried me in the house while I pretended to be asleep until I was well into the sixth grade, and who was ALWAYS the first person I called to deliver exciting news.

This was a man who took his youngest grandson everywhere with him despite there being whispers about my sister having a baby so young, who accepted folks in our church (despite strong opinions from some elders) because "God didn't give him a heaven or hell to put anyone in." A man who knew everyone by name at our local convenience store—and the names of their kids, too—and who everyone stood a little straighter for when he walked in. A man whose funeral was standing room only, even out in the foyer. A man's man. A great man.

I was devastated to lose him—the same man I spent 30 years clumsily trying to emulate—and I soon took on more responsibility for Red and our family. Suddenly, "she's her father's daughter" took on a whole new meaning. Months later, I filed for divorce and moved in with the only family I had in Chicago. I prayed I would figure out some way to stay in the city I loved while also caring for my family. This was my scariest step yet into the unknown.

Manifestation is Real

One year later, I was grateful to be safe and have my best friend's support as I decorated my tiny Chicago apartment. While still drowning in grief, I left the law firm to focus on my design business. However, I quickly grew tired of selecting beige sofas for clients who'd hired me simply because they wanted "something different." Meanwhile, I couldn't enjoy my morning chai without the New York Times or Harvard Business Review reminding me of my new crush: software.

I impulsively applied for an editor role at a tech research analyst firm. Then I put a post-it on my fridge with three bullet points relating to my new dream career:

1. A salary that would enable me stay in Chicago.
2. An opportunity to learn from female leaders.
3. A flexible schedule.

I read that post-it out loud every day and soon learned my first tangible lesson regarding the power of manifestation.

Keep in mind, I knew nothing about procurement tech. This was me taking yet another big step into the unknown. I just knew I wanted to live in Chicago while also securing my family's future, and to do so I had to make a change. I did my best to prepare and told myself this editor role was a good way to secure a bird's eye view of a very niche space in tech while also learning directly from industry leaders.

The founder of the tech research analyst firm got halfway through my third interview before pivoting to questions about executive client management. Somehow, I ended up landing an entirely different role, one that included everything on my post-it. I should've been thrilled, but I was scared shitless. Let me reiterate: I knew *nothing* about procurement tech. Nada.

I hired a college kid to show me how to use my new MacBook. When I showed up to my first team meeting, I was the only one with a notepad and pen. I had no idea what WordPress or CRM were, let alone what "contingent workforce" or "VMS" meant. Even though I was blessed with my father's quick wit and Red's intuition, I felt like a dinosaur. I was barely in my mid-thirties, yet here I was with that same feeling I'd had countless times as a kid—I was doubting myself, doubting whether I belonged.

Intention and Execution Will Make It Happen

For nearly a year, I read our clients' websites and watched industry-related videos for hours each week. I'd Google terms my younger counterparts were freely tossing around. School always came easily to me, but this? This was hell.

The only way to grow more confident (and thus more comfortable in your own skin) is to try new things.

Looking back, I realize that completely starting over at such a fragile point in my life was the bravest thing I've ever done. I learned there are no shortcuts to growth. The only way to grow more confident (and thus more comfortable in your own skin) is to try new things. And I mean *really* try. Like, potentially fall flat on your face in front of strangers with your heels kicked off and mascara running down your face. That kind of try.

I eventually was able to open my MacBook without experiencing a surge of anxiety. I had found my footing, so I turned my focus toward more strategic programs for my clients. When I was most scared, I'd turn my fear into fuel by reminding myself, "I'm doing this because I want to leave 'em better than I found 'em. My intention and execution will make it happen." That is still my mantra to this day.

I also had great clients: execs, sales, and marketing folks from all around the world who believed in their technology and their team. Their resilience and knowledge were my daily inspiration to do more and be *better*. I began managing their renewals, which translated to learning sales and introducing new products and processes.

The industry's premier marketing firm had an emerging female leader. At a client meeting one day, we met. She was tough, but also as innovative and honest as they come. Others clearly felt the same way about her. Soon after, she took an incredible new job opportunity at the leading global software provider for staffing and recruiting. A few months later, we had lunch.

Months of introductions, industry events, and phone calls later, I was back in Ohio for the holidays. I shared with my family the news that I was taking a new role in enterprise sales to learn from that same emerging female leader and other incredibly talented, well-respected people. Red's immediate reaction of anxiety, which my ego perceived as doubt, made me realize something that has stuck with me ever since:

When you take a big step into the unknown, you must look in the mirror and place your bet on YOU. Not even your mother, your closest sibling or confidant, will fully understand.

Or as my father would say: "Everything ain't for everybody." I wasn't certain this next move was the best for me, but I recognized the decision to trust my gut. This was *my* calling, not a conference call.

The one person I trusted to understand—my dear friend, Jess— came by later that week. We'd been through so much together as kids: her sleeping over at my house because her mom's boyfriend had become too much to handle, then my parents' phone ringing because her mother had died while he was drunk driving. Fifteen years later, she'd snuck in wine to the hospital while my dad lay dying and then held my head in her lap after I buried him. We had been each other's constants for so long.

When I pulled Jess aside to tell her my news, she jumped up and ran to her bag. She pulled out a black beaded bracelet with a single white bead to give me and showed me her matching white bracelet with a single black bead. "These are distance bracelets," she explained. "No matter where we are, you'll know that I'm with you and I'm rooting for you. Always."

I recognized a sadness in her eyes she could never quite hide from me, but I'll never forget how wide her always-perfect smile was in that moment. We had exchanged many gifts over the years, but never on Christmas. She assured me this wasn't a gift at all—it was her way of saying, "I love you."

The next day, my family had just sat down to open gifts when Jess' best friend began calling me. I answered after her first few tries to tell her I'd call back, but before I could say a word, I heard her sobbing. Jess was gone.

Later, I discovered she had left us each a voicemail that night saying she loved us. I played that message countless times between visits with her sister, hugs with her beautiful children, and my many hours spent writing the eulogy for the sweetest soul I had ever known. I don't remember a single word I said the day of her funeral except for a quote from Maya Angelou: "If you only have one smile in you, give it to the people you love."

That's what Jess did for me and everyone she loved. She gave us her smile and shared her light. Even on her darkest days. She left all of us better than she found us. I will strive to pay that forward for the rest of my life.

Trust Yourself to Trust Others

Two weeks later, I took a trip to London to join my new team for their annual kick-off meeting. The only person who knew about Jess was the woman who had recruited me. It felt unreal to trust her with something so personal. I especially feared that strangers might feel sorry for me or judge Jess' actions. Still, I chose honesty over pride.

She held my secret close. And in the following months, I learned to trust others and their intentions in a way I had never dared—all because I finally had the confidence needed to trust *myself*. I knew I could fall apart and find my way back, decide what and who was best for me, approach each moment with gratitude, and have faith when I needed it most. I vowed then to recognize that trust—in myself and others—was sacred. I would reciprocate that trust to anyone who showed it wholeheartedly to me.

The best part of my new mindset? I discovered that my passion had always been *people*. Helping them sell their business or choose a sofa was simply a way for me to express my greatest motivation: leaving 'em better than I found 'em. Or at the very least, being there for people as they find their own way—just as my father and Jess had always done for me.

Nearly two years later, there I was walking downtown in my new camel wool coat with ice-cold toes and tears of gratitude. When I reached State Street, my mind felt clearer than it had in months. Light snow began to fall—as if on cue—and I once again remembered the young Black girl who fell in love with a city, bet on herself, and took the first step of many that would lead me to where I am now.

I found myself thanking my mom for loving me even though she didn't grow up feeling loved or knowing how to love herself. I thanked my father for leading with character, Jess for trusting in me to share her smile with the world even after she was gone, and all of them for leaving me better than they had found me. Finally, I did something I'd never done before.

I thanked myself.

I thanked myself for making such an incredible decision so many years ago. For forgiving myself whenever I made a misstep. For continuing to make decisions for myself that my mother or grandmother never had the opportunity to make. And for realizing through it all that, to be truly grateful, I had to love myself enough to create a life I was proud of. By doing that, the young women in my life will hear my voice long after I'm gone. They'll know that they are loved and more deserving than ever.

I pulled my scarf tighter and glanced into a store window before crossing the street to hail a cab. My face was nearly covered, but I could still see in the reflection a woman who belonged exactly where she was. I couldn't help but wave and smile as I admired her beautiful new coat.

Kendra Cato

Kendra is a master connector and a fierce leader who drives results by understanding others at the deepest level. An energetic and analytical services professional with nearly 20 years of sales, marketing, research, and executive-level client management experience, she has held strategic leadership roles in industries spanning from investment banking and corporate law to procurement and talent management software.

Curiosity led her to earn a bachelor's degree from the E.W. Scripps School of Journalism at Ohio University, and she has loved getting to the bottom of things ever since. Since joining Bullhorn in 2018, she can usually be found learning from the leaders of the largest and most innovative staffing and recruiting firms across the globe, implementing new initiatives to scale the enterprise business, or discovering how the latest trends may impact the industry and the future of work.

Kendra's favorite sounds are a stamp on her passport, the pop of champagne, and the laughter of little ones. When home in Chicago, there's nothing she enjoys more than breaking bread with friends she considers family or curling up with a good book and her little dog, Kali.

Her passion is people, and she is grateful each day for the opportunity to impact lives through her work within the staffing and recruitment industry. She is active in the American Staffing Association (ASA) and Staffing Industry Analysts (SIA) as a member and speaker, and she's a proud council member of the ASA Inclusion, Diversity, and Equity Advocacy (IDEA) Group. Kendra is especially passionate about lifting up women and young Black professionals in the industry and beyond.

https://www.linkedin.com/in/kendracato/
https://twitter.com/kendracato

JUST TAKE OFF THE SHIRT

Beth Delano

Memories are funny. Something inside our brain picks and chooses what we remember. Sometimes the memory is perfectly clear. Other times it's a little fuzzy around the edges. I believe one of my earliest memories is what set me on course for my life.

I grew up in a small, Midwest Indiana town as the second-oldest of six kids in a strong Catholic family. I'm not sure how old I was—probably six or seven—but I remember the day like yesterday. It was HOT and MUGGY. The kind of muggy where your clothes stick to your skin. The sun was descending, and the neighborhood pack of kids were organizing another game of hide and seek. After one round, we all gathered together. We were huffing and puffing and dripping with sweat. Dust had turned into mud and was streaking down the sides of our faces.

I distinctly remember looking around and realizing that all the boys were standing around with their shirts off. For whatever reason—probably because I was so uncomfortable—it occurred to me that boys and girls abided by different sets of rules.

The next-door neighbor walked out to see what we were all up to. I looked up at him with indignation, then declared it wasn't fair that the boys didn't have to wear shirts while I did. He shook his head and chuckled, "Beth, that's just the way it is."

So, I took off my shirt.

That day seriously impacted my trajectory as a woman. I recognized there were unspoken rules, and that it was up to us to decide if certain rules fit our lives or not. We must consciously decide to move forward. In that moment, I took off my shirt. And later in life, when I had small children and was advised not to work extra hours or travel, I found a way to have the kids taken care of and still gave it my all at work. This allowed me to get additional responsibility, be noticed for my accomplishments, and eventually get promoted. I didn't do it for the sake of a promotion, I did it for my family and my kids. Wait—isn't that what men are encouraged to do?

Oh gosh, don't get mad at me! I'm not a radical feminist, but I used to be one when I was 18, 19, 20. I was radical, but I also had a very wise professor in college who told me, "Radicals don't get anything accomplished." I'm sure he said more to flesh out his point, but what stuck with me was this: If I wanted to create change for women in our society, being an extremist would not get me anywhere. I had to be the change in my own life.

You Own Your Career Path

I married at 21. We had our first child two years later, before I finished college. After I graduated, we moved to Bloomington, Indiana so my husband could finish his degree. I had wanted to go to graduate school to get my PHD and become a college professor. Instead, I needed a job while he completed his degree. Sometimes life is just like that—you've got to work to support your family by taking a job that might not be your first choice! But there also comes a point in everyone's life when you begin to make career decisions based on your personal goals. That is when you start owning your career path.

Write down your goals! You don't have to show anyone. Your list of goals can be your secret, or you can shout it out to the world.

Consider what steps you need to take to reach your career goals. My first goal after graduating college was to get a job. I remember getting dressed up and telling my husband, "I'm not coming home until I have a job!" That might not sound like a very lofty goal, but this was back during an era when we had more job seekers than job opportunities. Employers were picky.

I was new in town, so I sounded cocky declaring that I would get a job. Many hours and submitted applications later, I found myself at a department store accepting an offer for $8.25/hr. Honestly, I felt like I'd hit the jackpot! I had set a goal and achieved it! BOOM!

Here were my initial career goals:

1. Don't come home until you have a job.
2. Get accepted into a manager training program.
3. Get promoted.
4. Get promoted again.
5. Find a new industry to work in so I can have a better work/ life balance for my kids.
6. Make $50k a year.

You get the picture. Just write it down!

Your direction might change over time, and that's okay. When I started college, I wanted to be a journalist. Then I wanted to be in the FBI. Then I wanted to be a lawyer. Then I wanted to be a college professor. None of those things happened. But my determination—and the fact that I constantly set goals—moved me through each step of life. When I look back now, I notice how working towards each of those goals ultimately helped me recognize what I do and don't enjoy.

You Will Make Mistakes

Everyone makes mistakes. Isn't that what you've always been told? So, why don't we believe it? The important thing is to not let those mistakes define or derail you. What looks like a mistake in the moment might be the steppingstone you need for your next move.

My first staffing role was with Manpower (a global leader in the staffing industry). I was so blessed to start my staffing career with them because the training and structure were impeccable. I worked there for twelve years, starting out as a Branch Manager and ending as a Regional Director.

When I left Manpower, I took a position as an Enterprise Account Manager in a different industry in Atlanta, Georgia. My kids had already relocated once. They were devastated to be moving again. They were in fourth, seventh, and eighth grade. It makes me sick thinking back on it. Why did I think moving again was going to be a good idea? My kids rolled with it, but I could tell they were unhappy.

> *The important thing is to not let those mistakes define or derail you. What looks like a mistake in the moment might be the steppingstone you need for your next move.*

I ended up not really liking that job. I was mostly working with clients on conference calls, and I missed the in-person connection. The money was more than I ever thought I would make, but it wasn't worth everyone being unhappy. It was at this point in my career that I gained the courage to ask for what I deserved in compensation. So, when I asked the kids where they wanted to move next, we all agreed to go back to Louisville, Kentucky.

Let me back up a bit. It might sound like I was making a huge mistake. But for my career and our family's income, it wasn't. I took the job in Atlanta specifically because I wanted to gain C-level selling experience. As a Regional Director at Manpower, I knew I wouldn't be able to move into a corporate sales role and make more money without higher level selling experience. So, even though Atlanta didn't work for my family and seemed like a big mistake at the time, it ended up being the right move for my career. I would have never been considered for my next role as Vice President of Sales back in the staffing industry in Louisville. I certainly would not have had the training, experience, or guts to ask for proper compensation in my next role.

Owning your career path doesn't just mean setting your goals and accomplishing them. You must be thoughtful and intentional with your career. That means surrounding yourself with people you can rely on for honest, candid feedback.

When we moved back to Louisville, I attended an industry-related meeting where the keynote speaker shared some ideas on creating your own personal board of directors. This was another turning point in my career. We were encouraged to compile a group of individuals with diverse backgrounds and experiences. This meant our friends, coworkers, or acquaintances whom we respected and met with regularly to talk about challenges or to ask their advice. A crucial aspect of this structure was that you had to tell these people that you had selected them to be on your board of directors. You had to tell them you respected their opinion and that you would be calling on them from time to time for their viewpoint.

I scheduled to meet with each of the individuals I thought would provide me valuable insight. One person laughed so hard when I told him, but that was okay—he laughed often anyway. We became closer friends and have remained close to this day. Over the years, we shared our struggles as leaders and parents. He has taught me so many life lessons. He slowed me down when I found myself so often charging ahead.

It's Not Just About Women

Diversity has always been important to me. I remember when I was 16, sitting in the family room at Christmas. The lights were dim, and the Christmas tree lit up the room. I was snuggled up on the loveseat, and warm scents of baked goods spread through the entire house. I sat there journaling, with tears running down my face. I wrote about the racial inequality I saw all around me. It frustrated me how I had no control over it. I wrote about searching for a solution and a meaningful change in the world.

As a leader, I could begin changing the world and impacting those around me. As a Branch Manager, I had my team take an Understanding Poverty class. And as a Regional Director, I was proud to have a truly diverse team. Each leadership role allowed me to decide on hiring and the culture of my team.

Later in my career, when I was traveling in Jackson, Mississippi, the topic of inclusion was presented to me. I had randomly attended a local Society for Human Resource Management (SHRM) meeting. The speaker changed the direction of my career and gave me a whole new perspective on diversity. My coworker and I were running late after spending the morning canvassing a new territory. So, we didn't belong to this group—we were a couple of strangers walking in late. The speaker was the Chief Diversity Officer for a hospital group in Jackson. For thirty minutes, she spoke about diversity and inclusion. She painted a picture that I had somehow never seen. Suddenly, my eyes opened wider, and I finally understood! Just having a diverse workforce with fair and equitable pay is not enough; if people don't feel included, your job is not finished.

Create a culture that allows everyone to show up as their authentic self. When I returned from this trip to Jackson, I was fired up and ready to share my newfound direction. And while it was initially just tolerated by leadership, it was celebrated and embraced by the staff.

People won't feel connected to or accepted by an organization if they can't be themselves at work. That's the *truth*. I thought I was leading an organization that celebrated diversity, but I was wrong. As CEO, I didn't even feel comfortable showing up as my authentic self. I never shared personal details about myself because I thought I would be judged.

Shortly after my epiphany, we formed a Diversity, Inclusion, and Acceptance steering committee. It was incredible. The committee was all volunteer-based, and anyone who was interested (from within the entire company) could join. The input and ideas from the recruiters, on-sites, and branch managers was amazing! Our organization truly could become stronger and more diverse if everyone felt accepted for their talent and skill regardless of sex, religion, race, sexual orientation, socio-economic status, or anything else. If your staff can't come to work as themselves, they will never feel connected or accepted.

If You're Not Part of the Solution, You're Part of the Problem

I'm not telling you to rebel against societal norms. No, I'm suggesting that when you come up against something that doesn't seem right or fair, you say something. You have a voice. Find it. Use it. It is our collective responsibility.

If you recognize an unspoken rule that doesn't seem to fit ... say something.

If you have a career goal ... capture it.

If you make a mistake ... admit it and move forward.

If you see an opportunity to talk about diversity and inclusion ... speak up.

This is how we *all* get ahead. This is how women rise up. This is how we all get better—one voice at a time.

Beth Delano

Beth Delano started in the staffing industry in 1999 with Manpower. She was looking for a Monday-Friday, 8-5 job that would allow her to balance her work and home life, as raising her three kids was of the utmost importance.

Starting as a Branch Manager and ending with Manpower as a Regional Director, she went on to become an Enterprise Account Manager at SHL. After one year, she returned to the staffing industry with Malone Workforce Solutions, where she stayed for eight years and rose to the position of Chief Executive Officer.

With her kids now fully grown, Beth lives in Chicago, Illinois and serves as the Chief Operations Officer for Paramount Staffing (which is the North American arm of PROMAN Group, headquartered out of France). Beth is passionate about diversity and inclusion in all aspects of life. Her happy place is on the side of a mountain, taking a break from hiking to sit and admire the beauty of the earth.

https://www.linkedin.com/in/beth-delano-8859a05/

RAISING STRONG WOMEN –
THE ROLE OF A LIFETIME

Rhona Driggs

I am a single mom by choice. By age 37, I had accomplished everything I'd set out to achieve in my career, but I still had one more unfulfilled dream: I wanted to be a mom. I'd held many titles in my career—leader, mentor, boss—but the title I still craved was that of "mother."

I was divorced, single at the time, and not getting any younger. I didn't believe in the stereotype that you needed to be a wife to be a mom. And today, I hold the most important role I've ever had—that of a mother, role model, and mentor to my two beautiful daughters. I'm constantly thinking about the legacy I will leave them, so I'd like to dedicate this chapter to them. I want my lessons to be shared not only with them, but with all women who dare to be different.

Resilience Makes You Stronger

My parents divorced when I was five years old, after which I was raised solely by my mom. Growing up, we constantly struggled to make ends meet. We were extremely poor. I remember helping parent my younger brother as my mom worked three jobs to ensure we had food on the table. I was the peacemaker and caretaker in the family at a very young age. Just as I was graduating from high school, my father started spiraling down the path of drug addiction. He ended up losing everything he owned.

By the time I started college, I was working two jobs and trying to keep up with my scheduled classes. My dad was struggling physically and financially. He didn't have anywhere to turn. Being the eldest of the two children, I felt the need to become his caretaker, which was a familiar role for me. I ended up sacrificing my college education to help support him financially. While I was helping my father through drug addiction counseling, I realized that caretaking was a codependent behavioral trait. That was a turning point for me—what I needed most was to take care of "me" first.

Determination — You Have to Start Somewhere (Even If It's Not Glamorous)

My first job was in the fast-food industry. Doesn't everyone start in fast food? I could legally work at age 14, and I was determined to get a job so I could have my own money (I desperately wanted designer jeans!). On my 14th birthday, I took the bus to Burger King to put in an application. By the end of the day, I was employed. That was the start of my "career" journey.

> *I have always believed that 80% of success comes from having a positive mental attitude. This will help you overcome your fears and lead to greater success in life.*

I hated my job after the first two months, but I couldn't afford to leave before I had another job lined up. I resigned on a Tuesday, and by the following Monday I was employed as a waitress at a restaurant. I loved the tips and the instant gratification of having cash in my pocket every day, which was so foreign to me. I was able to work 30 hours a week during high school, and by the time I graduated I was managing a staff of 50 at the restaurant. I had to learn how to lead very quickly, so I used my experience as a leader in my family. I knew some of the staff didn't appreciate having a 17-year-old telling them what to do or how to do it. I considered what it meant to be a good leader, and the only knowledge I could apply was to "lead how I wanted to be led." It was an intimidating but amazing experience for me. This was the role that led me to discover my passion: helping others rise up.

Optimism is Required

Believe in yourself, and don't be afraid to put yourself out there! Sometimes it's not what you know, but who you know. When I was 19, I was fortunate to have someone recommend me for an admin position at Honeywell. It was my chance to escape the crazy demand and schedule of the restaurant industry. The job description stated that you had to type 35 words per minute, and you had to pass a typing test. I couldn't type that well, and I'd never worked an admin role before. Suddenly, I began thinking: "I'm never going to get this role. What do I have to offer?" A voice in my head was filling me with negativity. But I *really* wanted (and needed) the job.

I started writing down what I had to offer: quick learner, self-motivated, easily adapts to change, determination to succeed, and most of all a positive mental attitude. It was my optimistic attitude that got me thinking, "What do I have to lose?" and "How will I know if I don't try?"

As luck would have it, the typing test room was booked for a meeting the day of my interview, so I was unable to take the test. I sold myself and my "soft skills" during my interview, and I was offered a role supporting the Sector Head of Engineering in R&D. I couldn't believe it—I was going to be earning almost $27,000 a year!

I gave my notice to the restaurant and started my new job two weeks later. I was carrying a full load of college courses in the evenings and was often working 10 to 12 hours a day. This lasted nearly nine months, but the pressure of managing school and my new job eventually became too much. I realized I had a great career opportunity at Honeywell, and because my father was dependent on me financially (I already had a mortgage in my name for his house by that time), I made the difficult decision to quit college and focus solely on advancing my career. It was the only logical choice I could make at the time, as the physical and mental burden of caring for my father, attending college, and working had simply become too much.

Ambition is Not Optional

I was always the first one to raise my hand to take on extra duties and responsibilities. I loved the challenge of learning new things. Looking back, these extra responsibilities and learning experiences are what I'd call my "volunteer work." A reward won't always come with additional responsibility immediately, but in the long run your "volunteer hours" pay off.

During my time at Honeywell, the higher-ups made a major IT decision in the Research Division to transition from their internal operating system to Macintosh. I took the initiative to learn how to use Macintosh to design and create very large and complex proposals for the engineering team. Shortly after, I was asked to lead the rollout Macintosh training classes to all the admin departments. I didn't know it at the time, but that became the skill that would lead to my first opportunity in the staffing industry.

Courage is Conquering Fear

I had an amazing six-year career at Honeywell, but I still held the full-time role of caretaker elsewhere. I had a husband, a great career, and a home, but I decided to risk it all—literally. At the time, I felt the only way to break away from my role as caretaker was to move away. I needed to do something that would force me to put myself first. Distance was the only way I could achieve that. My only criteria for where I would move was good weather. Having grown up in the Midwest, I craved year-round sunshine and access to the ocean. I researched what area had the best weather, and San Diego vaulted to the top of my list.

Honeywell had a location there, so I took a risk and asked my boss if he could help me get an interview. He personally made some calls, and next thing I knew I was booked on a flight to San Diego. He encouraged me to also look at other options while I was there, so I had three interviews scheduled during my two-day trip. I began seriously questioning myself as I sat in my hotel room packing for my flight home. I was thinking: "This was a good experience, but should I just go home and play it safe?" and "What if I fail?" By the time I'd boarded my flight home, I had offers from all three companies. It was meant to be.

I ended up accepting an amazing opportunity to start in the staffing industry with Kelly Services as an Office Automation Manager. I would be using the skills I had learned with Macintosh and applying those to help accelerate sales and train temporaries how to use Mac. I resigned from my position, filed for a divorce, packed up my belongings, and moved across the country. My mom thought I was having a midlife crisis at 25. I didn't have a place to live, didn't know a single person in San Diego, and had never been there aside from my brief trip for my interviews.

It was the beginning of my staffing career.

Drive Equals Persistence

Early on in my corporate career, I had to face the reality that most leadership positions required a college degree. I could either let that be an obstacle or a challenge; I chose the latter.

I had to set myself apart to move up within the company. I again volunteered to be on task forces, special committees, and to lead various initiatives and projects. I knew I had to overcome my lack of a degree, and the only way I knew how was to prove I had the skills, ability, and ambition to succeed. In the end, my "volunteer work" paid off. I spent six years at Kelly Services and was promoted five times. I always feared failure, but I never let that stop me.

I have always believed that 80% of success comes from having a positive mental attitude. This will help you overcome your fears and lead to greater success in life.

Never Underestimate the Power of a Mentor

Years later, a brief encounter on a Saturday afternoon changed my life forever. I met the person I'd have the honor and privilege of calling my mentor for the next 22 years.

During one of my last relocations with Kelly Services, I was moving back to San Diego and had an appointment to go see a condo for lease in the area. I had no idea at the time, but the gentleman who owned the condo happened to be Jerome Shaw, a Co-Founder of Volt Information Sciences. He started the conversation by asking me prospective tenant questions like, "What do you do for a living?" and "What's your income?" I told him I worked for Kelly Services, and he shot me a puzzled look.

I then explained that Kelly Services was a large international staffing company, and he said, "I know, I co-founded Volt." Next, he did what any great recruiter would do—turned the conversation toward my career. Before I knew it, I had a meeting with him and his SVP the following Monday.

It took Mr. Shaw nearly two years to recruit me, but I finally decided to risk the career I'd built at Kelly to open several new markets for Volt in the Midwest. I never ended up renting that condo, but I did get to spend the next 22 years working with the most incredible person I've ever known.

Mr. Shaw was an amazing leader, mentor, and friend. In many ways, he became the father figure I never had. Sadly, he passed away in 2018. I was humbled and honored to be asked by his sons to help deliver his eulogy at his memorial service. It was the most difficult loss I had ever experienced. I will be forever grateful for the impact he had on my life both personally and professionally. Because of him, my desire to be successful—and to make a positive impact on the world and in the business community—became stronger than it ever would've otherwise been.

Integrity is Non-Negotiable

Integrity means always being true to yourself, your beliefs, and your values. Always be honest, take responsibility for your actions, and keep your promises. Also, never be afraid to admit when you are wrong—after all, we're only human, and owning your mistakes takes courage and can be humbling. It is important to always be honorable and deal with conflict professionally and respectfully. Be the example you want to see, treat people how you want to be treated, and lead how you want to be led.

You Really Can Have It All

After nearly 31 years, I continue to do what I love. I'm still as passionate about the staffing industry as I was when I started. After all, the staffing industry is about helping people, and I have great experience as a "caretaker." I have been able to use that experience to give back to others in a much healthier way.

Life is hard work, and it can sometimes be even more difficult as a woman. Find your passion and follow it, no matter how difficult it may seem. When you encounter obstacles or challenges, you have a choice. You can either rise up, or you can surrender. It's not always about winning—it's about never giving up. If you fall, stand up, be brave, and keep going. Take risks, or you'll never know the opportunities you lost. Dream big and fight for it!

I am blessed to be able to share my story alongside the amazing female leaders in this book. Most of all, I am blessed to have the greatest and most fulfilling role I've ever had: "Mom." You really can have it all!

Rhona Driggs

Rhona Driggs is the Chief Executive Officer of Empresaria Group, a publicly listed global staffing specialist based in the UK. Empresaria operates across 6 sectors in more than 19 countries.

Rhona has over 30 years of experience working in international companies within the staffing sector. She has a proven record of delivering growth and driving innovation. She has been recognized the past six consecutive years as one of Staffing Industry Analysts' Global Power 150 Women in Staffing. She was also named in 2020 and 2021 as one of Europe's Top 100 Most Influential Leaders in Staffing. She is recognized as a thought leader in the sector, with in-depth knowledge of contract/permanent staffing, MSP, RPO, and offshore recruitment.

Rhona is passionate about supporting the advancement of women in business. She is a member of the Women Business Collaborative (WBC) Advisory Council, an organization that strives to achieve equal position, pay, and power for all businesswomen. She is also an active member of several industry groups advocating for women in staffing and supporting DE&I (Diversity, Equity, & Inclusion).

Rhona's most important role is being a mother to her two teenage daughters.

https://www.linkedin.com/in/rhonadriggs/

INNER SUPERPOWERS

Anna Frazzetto

What drives me? What gives me the inner strength or superpowers needed to tackle the challenges of life? When pondering those questions, I pause and think about my childhood.

I was the third child to my parents, who migrated from Sicily in 1958. They came to America with my oldest sister. She sadly died as a three-year-old—from a tonsil operation—six months after arriving. My mom wanted to go back to Sicily, but my dad was determined to make it in the United States no matter what. Two years later, they were pregnant again—but they lost their second child to a still birth. They had to suffer through a full burial service in 1960.

Devasted by both tragic losses, my mom was determined to go back to Italy. But my father had the inner strength they needed to stay in America. My mom progressively got worse mentally and was on suicide watch for an extended period. My father decided to take her away to the Catskills—a big splurge for them—and happily, I was conceived there. Thus, the third child was born to Ines and Gaetano Frazzetto.

For the longest time, my parents thought they would be forever alone in this foreign country. Luckily, I was born on a beautiful spring day in the month of March. There's an expression Italians use to describe March: "Marzo e' Pazzo." That means "March is Crazy" and typically refers to the weather, but in this case my father used it about me, saying to my mother, "Ines, we're going to have our hands full with this March baby." I share this history because I strongly believe it shaped the fabric of my being. My determination and passion to survive and succeed come from my parents.

Accepting Who You Are

When you're a first-generation child of immigrant parents, your survival training begins immediately. And as a child of immigrants, you're given a passion to excel in life and tools to handle adversity and anxiety.

I grew up being the family translator. I would write out my father's invoices, pay the family bills, and handle any appointments or family transactions. Imagine being 10 years old, barely able to read and write in my third language, English, and having to understand tailor terminology or financial terms needed for writing checks and doing the family banking. I was put in a situation where I needed to grow up and mature quickly, which helped me learn the importance of family and the value of pulling together. My parents tried to learn proper English—they went to night school when they first got here—but with the tragedy of losing their firstborn and their difficulty conceiving again, they dropped out. So, when I was born, I learned how to speak Italian and Sicilian before English. I started kindergarten without a clue as to what everybody around me was talking about. I was a foreigner in my own country. My parents eventually hired a tutor, but I remember being totally horrified by school as a five-year-old.

A funny aside: when my mother first got here, she figured she would venture out and familiarize herself with the New York City neighborhoods. As she was walking, she noticed the word "SALE" written in big letters on several storefront windows. She found it odd because "SALE" was the Italian word for "salt." My mom returned home, and that night asked my father why salt was being sold at so many stores. To this day, the word "sale" brings joy to my heart—not because of the potential sale discounts, but because of how innocently my mother was trying to fit in, in America.

Because English was not my first language, I was always behind in school. My learning comprehension was always a grade or two behind. Luckily, with tutors and additional help, I excelled academically later in life.

When I was working my first job, I didn't fully understand what diversity meant or why it was so important. As I continued experiencing work and life, I realized I lived amongst diversity. There was a special bond shared in Lower East Side Manhattan. Our quest for prosperity united all of us. I was surrounded by Latinos, African Americans, Chinese, all of whom were looking to improve their lives. I never viewed us as being different or diverse; we were just families trying to make it.

When I was in high school, I began noticing how Italian my lunches were. I ate meals like veal parmesan or mortadella with provolone. I was mortified because my lunch always smelled funny. All I wanted was a PB&J or a ham and cheese sandwich. Oh, and my clothing clearly wasn't American either. I had to beg for my first pair of jeans, and I was in college when I finally got them. I was different—I didn't fit into what America deemed normal back then. It's amazing how being different caused me angst as a child, but today I embrace it. It made me who I am.

Family Ties

I value the impenetrable family bond we had growing up. Four years after my birth, my mom had another girl—my sister, Sandra. She was the apple of my eye. I took the responsibility of being an older sister seriously. I helped with feedings, diaper changes, and nap time. She was precious to me.

Our family unit was always strong, and we had dinner together nightly. My dad worked three jobs, meaning we had late dinners. But it didn't matter—it was crucial that we all ate together. My mom would get us from school and give us a hearty snack, then we would wait for dad to come home. There were no TVs or phones at dinner, just conversation. We would go around the table and tell dad what we learned at school, what we liked, what we were afraid of, and what we were looking forward to the next day. We grew up poor, so we had to create our own fun. We always had our theater and show nights, where my sister and I—plus my two cousins—would perform for our parents. We'd sing a song, act a scene out, or dance the latest craze.

The one thing my husband, Bob, always found remarkable was that the four of us (myself, my sister, and my cousins) all graduated from college. It was odd to him because our parents had elementary school degrees at best. So, how could these children of immigrants excel academically? Because of my father. He was ahead of his time, and he always encouraged us to be independent and go to college.

I have vivid recollections of how strong the community ties were in my neighborhood. We were all there for a common goal: to provide for our families.

At the dinner table, my dad had a rule that mom would only prepare one meal. Whatever it was, we had to eat it and be grateful she prepared it for us. One night, my mom made broccoli soup and added mozzarella and pasta to it. It was delicious, but my sister wasn't enjoying it. So, she asked mom for something else. (Since my sister was a picky eater, my mom was always worried she wasn't eating enough—classic Italian mom.) My mom was about to get up to make something else, but my dad did not allow it. He told my sister she had to eat her bowl of soup. My sister said no, and my dad said, "You're not getting up till you eat it, or else you'll be wearing it." I sat there with my mouth agape, wondering what my dad was going to do. My sister was strong-willed, and she wasn't budging. Next thing I knew, my dad leaned over and dunked her face in the soup bowl. I was shocked, she was hysterical, and my mom simply began cleaning up. Since then, no one ever questioned what we were having for dinner.

My dad was a strong, dominant figure. It always impressed me how he commanded the room. Even when we were struggling to make ends meet, he maintained his confidence.

Turning Fears to Strengths

The fear of failure is woven into the fabric of my being. My dad was driven by it too. We never discussed it later in life, but it was clear to me because of how he operated in life and how he always encouraged his children. From when my mom wanted to go back to Italy after losing a child right up until his final days, it was always there. He wanted to make it in NYC, and as the song goes: "If I can make it there, I can make it anywhere."

There are a few moments that stick out when I look back upon my life-altering experiences. One was when I almost drowned at Jersey Shore as an 11-year-old. I had to be rescued by lifeguards, and to this day I have a fear of drowning. Another came during the 9/11 crisis, when I had to lead my team back home and to safety. We had our annual operations team meeting in Lyndhurst, NJ, and we witnessed the attack on the Two Towers across the river from our office windows. Immediate panic made everyone want to be with their families, which wasn't easy because all airports were shut down and car rental places didn't want to release cars if they were being dropped off in different states. It was traumatic watching how it impacted everyone differently, and I had to be sensitive to their needs and ensure they got home safely from work.

The first time I had to terminate someone is another moment I recall. It was very different from my last termination. With my first termination, I second guessed every move I made. I wondered why I was letting this person down. Today, I recognize you can lead a horse to water, but if they are not willing to put in the effort, they are basically terminating themselves.

My fear of failure has shifted over the years. Now I'm driven by my inner confidence. Every life lesson has influenced and impacted my future growth. I often advise others to think about the decisions they make and reflect on how the outcomes impacted them. I believe that years of experience position you to lead others more naturally. Granted, this assumes you never stop learning, and you cherish each of your life lessons.

The Power of Mentors

I was significantly impacted by the death of my father in 2005. He died young, and I felt there was so much more I could have learned from him. He was my calming voice, my mentor, teacher, protector, and guide through life. How is it that someone who only graduated from elementary school could be so wise? As I said, he was ahead of his time, an early champion of "girl power." I'll never forget him telling me I could do whatever I wanted if I believed it. Now, when I mentor young salespeople, I tell them to set goals for themselves. "If you believe it, you'll achieve it." I say. And: "The only obstacle in your way is you."

When my father died, I was extremely lonely and lost. Who could I go to for advice? Who knew the right words to calm me and give me the confidence I needed to accomplish anything? My father taught me to let go of my fear of failure and come at it from a position of confidence and knowledge.

I've learned that mentors are essential. I was seeking mentors before the word "mentor" was even used at work. My father was my first mentor. He influenced everything about me, and I am forever grateful for him and the journey we shared.

Equally important were the mentors in my work career, starting with Marty Tillinger of MHT Services. Marty recognized I was great in front of clients. He knew I couldn't be a tech nerd for the rest of my life. (I graduated with a double major in computer science and mathematics from NYU—two subjects that weren't popular for women when I went to college, but which my father encouraged me to go for. (When I graduated, I was one of two women to graduate with those majors.)

Later in life, I met a series of mentors: Michael Frank from Syncsort, Ira Goodman from Syncsort, Bill Frankhusen and Tom Martin from Comdisco, and Bob Miano. I later married Bob—some might say there is a Freudian message there because he's so like my father. Bob always encouraged me to tap into my inner strengths, and he positioned me well to follow my sales and business leader career. I am forever grateful for the mentor, leader, and husband he is to me.

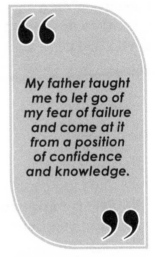

My father taught me to let go of my fear of failure and come at it from a position of confidence and knowledge.

These leaders helped me during my transition from tech wiz to sales wiz. I've loved every step of my journey, and I think my tech background helped me succeed in life. But if it wasn't for these individuals—all of whom helped me and guided me and basically told me I can do whatever I want to do—I'm not sure where I'd be. I am grateful to all of them, and that's partly the reason why I'm sharing my story in this book. I'm hoping my words can strengthen others and help them achieve whatever they desire, just like I did.

Stay True to Yourself

I always stay true to myself. If that means going against a popular vote, so be it. Starting out in a management career, it's easy to become a "yes" person because you want to be accepted as a new manager/leader. But being a "yes" person will only hurt you. My father used to call this the "look at yourself in the mirror" test. Years later, Bob told me the same thing. The test basically goes like this: If you look at yourself in the mirror, are you happy with what you see? Do you smile or look away? That's the key—you need that smile!

It's often challenging for new leaders to be self-aware. That's why second or third parties are important: they highlight what you might be missing. I'm a big fan of therapy, where you can expose your inner self to a professional. When you get to that raw state, you can learn from yourself and then positively impact your outcomes. When my first marriage ended in divorce, everyone told me to go see a therapist. "Why?" I thought. I was so happy to end that dead marriage. What could a therapist tell me that I didn't already know? Well (shocker alert), it was the best choice I ever made! I allowed myself to be vulnerable, and in doing so was able to address some fundamental issues I had been carrying with me since childhood. I had to fix these things before engaging in another marriage with Bob. Over the years, I have relied heavily on my inner circle of friends and family to help me and keep me on track. You must check your behavior at times, which might mean having hard conversations. But it's the only way you'll improve yourself and become a better leader.

At sporting or entertainment events, I often hear parents shouting to their children: "Be confident" or "Go get 'em" or "You got this!"

Well, I believe confidence is a learned skill; it does not come naturally. Maybe I'm wired differently, but I had to practice constantly at everything. As I improved, my confidence increased. I couldn't be confident in something until I'd put in the work. Of course, I grew up in a household that had two philosophies: 1) My mother thought that if you appeared perfect and strived for outer perfection, you could gain confidence; and 2) My dad was more focused on the practice part, not being perfect—he thought perfection would come with enough diligent practice. I chose to follow my dad's route because any time I tried to appear perfect, I would lose sight of what I was trying to accomplish.

Here's a bit more advice: when addressing others regarding any subject matter, make sure you have your facts straight and you've removed emotion from the conversation. This approach gives merit to your topic, and it will give you confidence to debate the matter diligently.

When I've been asked what I want to leave my nieces, nephew, or grandkids as far as life lessons or golden nuggets to success, I always answer with the following pieces of wisdom:

Be true to yourself, rely on your inner circle, and get a therapist when you need to! ☺

Confidence doesn't mean perfection, and it's fine to go against the grain. Don't be afraid to have a different opinion than others.

If you believe it, you can achieve it—AMEN!

Surround yourself with diversity—in thought, people, and your daily processes. Embrace things that are different.

Hang on to your roots. They are the DNA of life that make you unique and special. Don't try to blend into what everybody else is.

Focus on lifting each other up, not tearing others down. Support your colleagues—help them succeed. Don't focus only on yourself, as the world does not revolve around just you.

Hopefully you can apply these simple rules to drive your career and prosper in life's journey. Your success starts with your inner strength (SUPERPOWER). Remember to ignore all the negative banter around you or within you. Tap into yourself, and channel your SUPERPOWER.

Anna Frazzetto

Anna Frazzetto, a first-generation Italian American, shares the value of looking back to understand how the strength and persistence of our immigrant families shapes who we are today. At a time when diversity and inclusion remain elusive, our roots reveal the commonality of what our immigrant families worked for—a better life for their families, neighbors, and co-workers.

As a Senior Executive, Anna is a leader in executing IT solutions strategies. Her expertise in digital transformation and data analytics helps guide businesses of all sizes, from leading U.S. enterprises to fast-growing start-ups to global industry leaders. She is dedicated to helping organizations expand their digital capabilities, embrace innovation, and tackle business challenges across the technology spectrum. Frazzetto is also a sought-after speaker on digital innovation, outsourcing, and workplace diversity. She is an advocate for increasing the numbers and influence of women in technology. She is currently the national chair of ARA, an organization committed to attracting, retaining, and advancing women in IT.

Frazzetto has been on Staffing Industry Analysts' Global Power 150 Women in Staffing list five consecutive years (2017-2021). She is a regular contributor to CIO.com and sits on the Forbes Technology Council. She was also named to SIA's Top 50 DEI Influencers list in 2021.

Anna's daily passion is to create a more equitable world for future generations—including her nieces, nephew, and six grandkids.

https://www.linkedin.com/in/annafrazzetto/

EVERY DAY, CHOOSE YOU

Ericka Hyson

**"I love to see a young girl go out and grab the world by the lapels. Life's a bitch. You've got to go out and kick ass."
Maya Angelou**

As a child, I was painfully shy, reluctant to speak up or be the center of attention. My parents divorced when I was very young. I observed how my mother took charge of her future, decided what was best for herself and her family, and made whatever changes were necessary despite how difficult they may have been. My mom went from being a housewife in an unsatisfying marriage to becoming the first woman in her family to enroll in college. She pursued a career in fashion and retail management, raised her children, built a solid support system, met and married the love of her life, and continued to grow our family. While my mom was building a new life for herself—enrolling in college, starting a career, juggling getting two kids back and forth to school and sports programs—she leaned on her mother and best friend: my Gram.

Gram was our family's rock. She lost her first husband, my grandfather, to melanoma before I was born. As one of four sisters, she was raised during the Great Depression. She was surrounded by strong women. She went through so much yet was always a ray of sunshine and positivity. I'm eternally grateful that my mom and Gram had such a remarkable bond, and that Gram lived with us for many years. Her presence in the room was never missed. Always dressed to the nines, she was strong, supportive, loving, adventurous, and downright hilarious. She taught our family the importance of love, affection, and laughter. She spoiled us with her amazing cooking, creative energy, gratitude, and kindness until the day she died at 94. Gram taught me patience. She taught me to appreciate making things with my hands. She taught me to sew, paint, make pottery, garden, roller-skate, and appreciate the beauty of being outdoors and in nature. She was gentle, kind, and compassionate. She always supported and encouraged me, no matter what.

At the age of six, I proudly rocked my favorite 1970's style ringer t-shirt. The words "Girls can do anything boys can do, but better" were proudly displayed under the image of a young girl in pigtails riding her bike. It was a gift from Gram. This t-shirt inspired me to dream—could I do anything boys could do? Could I do it better? Yes! I was determined.

Growing up in Florida, I was very close and competitive with my older brother, who is two years older than me. Our parents divorced when I was six, and we would visit our dad every other weekend. I never wanted to be excluded from weekend activities with my dad and brother—I wanted to fit in. I learned to BMX, skateboard, boogie board, deep-sea fish, canoe, water ski, kneeboard, and snow ski with them. I watched football and cheered for my dad's favorite team. On Halloween, I steered clear of pretty princess costumes, choosing to dress up as the following characters instead: a gorilla, Private Benjamin, a railroad engineer, and the Wicked Witch of the West. I ran barefoot around the neighborhood with my hair a tangled mess. I played Rambo in ditches, skateboarded, and BMX dirt biked. I was relentless in my pursuit to do anything boys could do. I wanted to fit in and feel included.

I was a young girl when I realized women weren't afforded the same privileges as men. I thought being more like the boys would mean being treated equally. I remember my mom telling a story about going door-to-door to collect signatures (with me in a stroller). She was petitioning to stop the rezoning of a very large, tree-covered, Florida riverfront parcel, which was being zoned from residential to a high-density unit development. She was very successful in getting signatures and getting homeowners to pack City Hall in protest. Afterwards, the president of the newly formed local homeowner's association, a retired Colonel, told her, "Wow, Cindy. You impressed the hell out of me. Do you think your husband would sit on our Board of Directors?" How infuriating!

It's no wonder I loved reading stories about badass women like Harriet Tubman and Harriet Jacobs. They fought for freedom and their families in the face of adversities I could never fully comprehend. I became determined. My life would somehow be different, and I was inspired by my mom, my Gram, and these brave historical women to believe in hope and the opportunity to level the field. Along with learning about inequalities women face, my childhood experiences taught me that change can be both difficult and empowering. There is power and strength in women supporting women.

The matriarchs in my family taught me resilience, strength, and adaptability. By the time I started college, I resolved to never depend on a man for anything. Determined to live on my own and support myself, I worked full-time in retail store management, insisting that I pay for my room and board while attending the College of William and Mary in Virginia.

After college, I moved to Charlotte and continued my career in retail management. One day, I learned of an amazing opportunity to be a technical recruiter for a start-up staffing company, ettain group. I joined ettain group in January of 1999 with little knowledge of computers and very sparse hands-on experience with software. Despite being one of the first women hired in the company, the founding partners—Jeff, Brian, Rob, and Jon—warmly welcomed me to the team. They played instrumental roles in my career growth. As an English Literature major, I had zero experience in recruiting, staffing, or technology. But they took a chance on me. I instantly fell in love with everything about the opportunity—the people, the independence, the opportunity to learn and grow and be rewarded for my successes, the support to try new things and innovate, and the chance to take on new roles and create opportunities for others. I was inspired daily by the rapid pace of technological advancement, the people I met, and the relationships I built with talent, clients, and teammates.

Being a fast-growing start-up, there were always opportunities to take on additional responsibilities, ask for stretch assignments, and create roles for others. Throughout my 20-year tenure with ettain group, I held countless roles—from technical recruiting, leadership, sales, account management, branch management, internal talent acquisition, internal training & development, technology, and operations.

In my early years at ettain group, I was determined to be a top performer. I put my head down and assumed my hard work would be recognized and rewarded. I was never great at advocating for myself or asking for what I wanted. Instead of waiting to be tapped on the shoulder, I focused on mastering my current role, and I kept an eye on what I might want to do next. I took the initiative to learn new skills and take on additional responsibilities for the next role, and I simultaneously identified people in the organization whom I could mentor and develop to replace me. This strategy proved effective for my career advancement while simultaneously providing the platform to create opportunities for others across the organization. It allowed us to become more diverse and inclusive as an organization as we hired, developed, and promoted several generations of women in the organization.

No Time for Negativity

In 2009, I was pregnant with my son and operating in an executive leadership role with ettain group when our President, Rob, shared with me the news that would change my life forever. He had cancer.

Rob lost his battle to colon cancer two years later in February of 2011. He was larger than life, and so many other things—Partner and President of ettain group, my boss, mentor, and friend. He was respected by all and impacted so many people. To this day, he makes me want to be a better version of myself. He loved life and especially loved his family, his team, fitness, great music, fast cars, nice clothes, stylish shoes, cycling, and hot tamales. Since Rob's passing, I have gained so much perspective. Now I dare to share the incredible lessons I learned from him.

Rob would say the same thing to anyone who threatened to damper his positive vibrations: He didn't have time for any forces in his life aside from positivity, faith, hope, and love. He taught me the power of radiating light, love, and positivity—and how contagious it can be to the people around you.

Rob experienced many ups and downs during his fight with cancer. But rather than complaining or feeling sorry for himself, he would frame his setbacks as "speed bumps." He faced so many disappointments—like when he would come back from a doctor's appointment and learn that the results of his chemo weren't what he expected, or that he wasn't eligible for a clinical trial. Yet he never missed a day of work, and he never complained.

Rob's office was across the hall from mine. There were days when he would return after a treatment and push past his pain or fatigue. There were times when he was physically cold—a side effect from his chemo—and he would bundle up and make a joke about his fashionable fingerless gloves and hat. He was always smiling, refusing to invite negativity into the room.

Rob's tremendous courage and infectious positivity in the face of adversity have taught me that nothing should hold me back from following my passions. Nothing. And if things don't go as planned, I'll simply adjust the plan, chart a new course, and never give up. I can recognize now that there were many times in my career where

I brought stress upon myself. Sometimes to the point where I would become physically ill, and over trivial matters like deadlines or self-imposed pressure to perform. When I feel stressed now, I remind myself, "I don't have time for negativity." If my family and loved ones are healthy and happy, I have the power to choose to deflect the negative stressors in my life.

> **"He who knows others is wise; he who knows himself is enlightened." Lao Tzu**

Time is precious. If you knew today was your last day on earth, how would you choose to spend your time? What would you do differently? I recently started reflecting on these questions. What do I want? What lights the fire within me? I started journaling and exploring these ideas. It became clear I was doing some things to please others instead of prioritizing myself. I created a list of what is important to me, which has become my north star for pursuing my passions and honoring myself. I asked myself these questions and came up with the accompanying guidelines:

1. *Am I building something?*
   I want to have the autonomy to build something, try new things, and not fear failure.

2. *Am I surrounding myself with A players?*
   I want to be surrounded by great people who are passionate about growing, having fun, and raising the bar for others around them. They must be open, challenge each other, trust each other to try their best, and inspire others to bring out their best.

3. *Am I learning new things and solving complex problems?*
   I must continue to expand my skills and take on new problems to solve.

4. *How do I feel about what I give to the people closest to me?*
I want to give the best version of myself to my family, friends, and colleagues.

5. *Who has my best interest at heart? Who makes the decisions about me?*
It is important to be true to myself, no matter what.

I hang these in my office as a reminder that my dreams are important. I am worthy of the opportunity to chase my dreams.

Advocate For Yourself

Rob's battle with cancer taught me to step outside of my comfort zone and accept challenges head-on. There's a difference between being intentional and being opportunistic. Being intentional means you are in the driver's seat, playing an active role—setting goals, building a plan to achieve them, and executing. Being opportunistic means tagging along for the ride—a more passive approach.

As Rob was fighting for his life, I learned that I was my own best advocate. I couldn't waste any time or expect my hard work to be recognized. I couldn't simply wait for someone to tap me on the shoulder for the next opportunity. I learned the importance of advocating for myself, taking ownership of my personal growth, and asking for what I needed, however terrifying that might be. Really, what's the worst that can happen?

"I dwell in possibility." Emily Dickinson

Rob also taught me that even the biggest dreams have no limits. In February of 2011, a few weeks before he died, I asked him about his wishes and hopes for the future of the company. "What number would make you proud?" I asked. "$100 million," he whispered. "If *our competitor* can do it, so can we." He smiled.

In 2010, ettain group had closed at $48M in revenue. Rob's goal seemed so grand, almost impossible. Rob lost his battle to cancer a few weeks later. In the wake of this tragic loss, the team and I surprised ourselves in many ways. We stepped up, took on new responsibilities, and put our arms around each other to fill tremendously large shoes. And with that determination, we surpassed Rob's seemingly lofty revenue goal and exceeded $100M within a few short years!

Success built character and confidence. I found myself energized by the pace of growth, excited about the opportunity to innovate and scale the business, inspired by the strength and courage of the team, and more confident in the idea of infinite possibilities. In 2012, I took another giant step in my career (despite being terrified). With encouragement from Jeff, Brian, and Jon, I stepped into a new role as VP of People. I was tasked with building an internal People Department focused on internal customers—hiring, growing, developing, engaging, and retaining talent—which was vital to position ettain group for continued growth and scale.

> *Great support systems are invaluable. Giving and receiving are both essential. I learned how valuable it is to be both flexible and transparent as a leader.*

Fearful thoughts crept into my head: "What if I fail? What if I'm not taken seriously? What if I don't have enough experience? Am I even qualified for this?" I'd spent the previous 12 years focusing on acquiring, growing, and servicing external customers—talent and clients—but had no experience or formal training in traditional Human Resources roles. But I was confident in my abilities to reach even higher than what I'd previously dreamed possible. I silenced the voice in my head saying, "You need more experience. You've never done this before." Instead, I asked myself, "What if I try and succeed?" I embraced the idea that even the biggest dreams have no limits. I began to dwell in possibility.

COVID-19 might have made it easier for you to relate to this experience of doing extraordinary new things and coming out on the other side feeling more confident. So, what have you done to surprise yourself? How can you build on this foundational growth and take another step forward?

Give and Receive Support

Great support systems are invaluable. Giving and receiving are both essential. I learned how valuable it is to be both flexible and transparent as a leader. I've had the privilege to experience the magic that happens when dynamic, engaged teams rally to achieve a common goal and achieve results. Our team was stronger than any individual player could ever be. This came as no surprise, since we'd learned from Rob, who never tried to battle cancer alone. Instead, he established a robust team of experts across many fields, including doctors, oncologists, spiritual leaders, nutritionists, and of course, his incredible support network of family, friends, and colleagues. Rob's approach to battling cancer taught me the value of a diverse team. A tremendous support network will not only be by your side—they will also challenge you, present different opinions, and offer valuable perspectives.

This inspired me to surround myself with people who would challenge me, deliver hard truths, present fresh ideas, and show me different perspectives. I took it upon myself to create a personal team of advisors, mentors, and friends across many industries— individuals I now trust to challenge my thinking and help me identify blind spots. I can ask them, "What am I not thinking about, not seeing?" and expect an honest answer. Building this board of allies, mentors, and coaches has been invaluable to my career advancement and personal growth. I have learned the value of having more questions than answers—and above all else, that it's okay to ask for help.

Letting Go of Fear

Six months after Rob lost his battle to cancer, I received the same news from one of my oldest and best childhood friends, Norm. He had cancer.

Norm had just completed his Ph.D. program at UCLA and was beginning his career as a professor at Clark University in Worcester, Massachusetts. The diagnosis came just three weeks after his 38th birthday. He had been diagnosed with stage III malignant metastatic melanoma. After more than 17 surgeries, rigorous chemotherapy, systemic acupuncture therapy, and countless clinical trials, Norm lost his battle to cancer two years later in February of 2014, three years after Rob's passing.

That winter, I spent nearly every weekend visiting Norm in Boston. While his body was weak, his mind remained courageous, positive, strong, and determined. Like Rob, his commitment to sharing the gift of his time with his family, friends, and students was inspiring. He insisted on continuing to teach his students via Zoom while in hospice care. He had so much to give, and he poured all his last bits of life and energy into those he served. His desire to teach and create opportunities for others was truly inspiring.

Inspired by Norm's bravery, I had the confidence to accept the role as Chief Operating Officer of ettain group in January of 2014. As I considered the job, my internal voice was asking, "What if I didn't have any fear? What's the worst that could happen?" I reminded myself, "Choose You. Every day, choose you." I was determined to let go of my fears of failing. I was ready to accept any challenge with abundant confidence. I knew I had a great support team, and I reminded myself that the "stress" of learning new skills or fearing the unknown was a choice. I told myself the truth: I deserved the opportunity to chase my dreams.

Big Leap

By 2018, I had been COO for four years. I was proud of my accomplishments, our incredible team, and the contributions I had made for nearly 20 years to the growth and success of a great company. I revisited my five questions and realized it was time for a change. It was hard to admit, but I found myself too comfortable, suddenly craving bigger challenges and growth. I read my five questions again and again. Being brutally honest with myself was hard. I loved my company and my team, but I was also prepared to take a step that felt more like a giant leap.

This time, the voice in my head was saying, "I'm not done yet. My possibilities are infinite. I am worthy of chasing my dreams." So, that summer, I resigned after a two-decade run with ettain group, packed up my life of 25 years in Charlotte, and moved across the country to pursue a software career in Colorado.

The move has been transformative on so many levels. I've learned to let go of things to create room for new experiences, expand my network, challenge myself every day, and develop new skills. My family has become closer, and we are exploring the wonders of Colorado together. I find myself energized by spending more time outside—hiking, biking, skiing, or just stepping out into my yard and breathing in the fresh mountain air. I've been practicing letting go of many of the material possessions that once filled my closets—shoes, clothes, handbags—and embracing a simpler life. I have expanded my support system and embraced new friends both near and far. I have rekindled my love for sewing and have a newfound appreciation for handmade art. I'm creating space to give back, whether in the form of sewing masks for the local community or mentoring women in staffing and tech. I continue to stretch and grow.

Today, as President of WorkN, I am energized by being a part of such a fast-growing software company. We are providing innovation and improving customer experiences for the staffing industry I've come to know and love. It's incredibly rewarding to have the opportunity to build upon the foundational skills I have, and to expand and grow from experiences. As I reread my five questions, I am confident that I am exactly where I should be at this moment. And I am excited and optimistic about what the future holds.

Both Norm and Rob were one-in-a-zillion, larger-than-life individuals. My words alone can't do them justice. Witnessing their courage, tenacity, and strength has challenged my core personal beliefs. I am grateful for the life lessons I've learned, and I hope my story will inspire you. Listen to your voice and have the courage to follow your dreams. Your dreams and adventures are worth chasing. You are worthy of the opportunity to chase your dreams. The small steps will give you confidence and courage to take big leaps. Choose YOU, every day.

Ericka Hyson

Ericka Hyson is the President of WorkN. She brings over 21 years of combined experience as both an executive in the staffing industry and CX-tech industry. She has incredible passion and drive for leadership, innovation, building world-class service organizations, and leveraging mobile-first technology to deliver incredible customer experiences.

Hyson is a three-time honoree of Staffing Industry Analysts' Global Power 100 Women in Staffing list. This list recognizes and honors women around the globe who are thought leaders, passionate about promoting and shaping talent, and key influencers in the staffing industry.

Ericka was honored by the Charlotte Business Journal with the 2018 Women in Business Award. She currently serves on the Board of Directors for the Colorado Technology Association. She also volunteers for the ASA's Women in Leadership Council and non-profit organizations Girls in Tech and All-In to Fight Cancer. Ericka is a graduate of the College of William and Mary. She resides in Boulder, Colorado.

https://www.linkedin.com/in/erickabhyson/

BECOMING

Lauren B. Jones

"Breath in, breath out. Breath in, breath out."

I used to recite those words to myself as I drove through our idyllic NorCal suburb. I kept waiting for the heaviness in my chest to disappear, for the day I could breathe in a complete breath. I'd reached a level of discontentment that had left me searching for the proverbial itch to scratch.

From the outside looking in, we were a picture-perfect family: Mom, Dad, two beautiful girls, good jobs … living the American Dream. Our eldest daughter was off to college, and our youngest was in her sophomore year of high school. Things were going "swimmingly." There was no obvious reason to disrupt our current state. And yet, the itch could not be scratched.

I knew only a few things at the time: I needed space to breath, I needed to re-evaluate what was important to me, and I needed to have something other than work to define myself. The following existential questions began swimming around in my head, and I was desperate to get them answered:

Who am I really?
What work have I done to figure that out?
Do I like who I am?
Do I like the way my two daughters see me?
Do I like what I see when I look at my reflection? Not just on the outside, but on the inside.

For me, a change of scenery would create the spark I needed to gain some clarity. It was so obvious to me, but not to the rest of The Jones Clan. I won't forget the initial family discussions we had regarding a move. They shot me looks of disbelief, especially since I'm usually the one most resistant to change.

New property? Fixer upper? Good bones?

"Mom has lost her damn mind!"

Initially, the idea was met with significant pushback. But as we began looking at properties, I saw them slowly buying into the vision. Less house, more of that space I kept talking about. As my husband and I began to align in our vision, I felt a little like Dorothy from *The Wizard of Oz*—what was black and white was transitioning to color. Perhaps it was the risk, the excitement of taking control, or the connection it was creating for our family. Whatever it was, I felt reinvigorated.

The journey to find "space" was a long one. It took us about 18 months to find property in California that wouldn't require a 45-year mortgage, the exchange of my first-born child, and every penny we'd ever saved. But somehow, we eventually found it. The house had "good bones." It was in rough shape, a bare property with an old 1950's rambler on it. Yet, for some unknown reason, I remember walking up the sidewalk during our initial walkthrough and thinking: *This is the one.* If you've ever had a moment where you know you are EXACTLY where you're supposed to be, you know how life-affirming it can be.

But change isn't without doubt or reservation. Good people and good partners make all the difference. By then, my husband was one hundred percent onboard. And even though I had that life-affirming feeling, I was still scared. I hesitated, I started fights, and I tried to back out of our decision—all because of fear.

My gut knew how hard it would be to make the transition and renovate the home and land. My husband and I had committed to one another—we would do the work ourselves and do it without loans. Just our hard-earned cash. This meant I'd have to work on being patient, as I knew it wouldn't be an overnight process. Those who know me also know that patience is not a virtue I possess.

Lightening the Load

It's funny, when your life comes into focus, you begin to see things differently. What was once important becomes trivial. My personal life became crystal clear to me during this transition. I realized that the *space I so desperately needed had been taken up by material things and stuff.*

I had fallen into the trap of consumption and comparison. Constantly comparing myself to others, buying things I didn't need just to fit in. I looked for satisfaction and fulfillment in consuming. I ate too much, drank too much, and participated in too many toxic relationships. I was prioritizing quantity over quality, trying to impress people with my possessions. Trust me, that way of life will eventually weigh you down.

Our move would function as the catalyst I very desperately needed. I had to begin the process of lightening the load of bad priorities.

We had 12 days to move 15 years' worth of belongings from a 4000 square foot home to a 2200 square foot home. We could not find movers in that amount of time, so it was all on us. When you are faced with packing what's most important in very short timeframe—well, you realize how much unimportant garbage you've accumulated. What began as a painful exercise of ridding myself of "things" became one of the most rewarding and liberating experiences I can remember. It lit a fire of giving within me. Ultimately, I ended up donating most of my wardrobe away to Women's Empowerment in Sacramento. We sold almost all our furniture and donated an absurd amount of "stuff" to various organizations. And we haven't missed a single thing since!

The Journey is the Sweetest of All

When we pulled up to the new house, I finally took that unencumbered breath I'd been so desperately trying to take. My shoulders relaxed for the first time in ages.

But that solace was momentary, as I immediately began to feel a terrifying sense of buyer's remorse: "What have I done? What are people going to think? How will I explain? What if they don't see our vision? It's never going to be done." Mind you, we hadn't even started. My initial doubts came flooding back and I was in full-on panic mode.

Maybe you're wondering: "Why the hell would you care what other people thought of you? And why did you care whether or not they knew about your vision?" I don't have good answers to those questions. It's taken a lot of time and growing up to get past what other people think, and I've put in some *serious* work on my confidence. To get past this panic, I did the only thing I knew how to do at the time, which was to put in the work. Work on the house, work on work, work on me—DO THE WORK.

This time was no different. We worked on our labor of love constantly. Every waking moment was a project, a task, a planning session. We planned to live in the house while we renovated, so we played musical rooms and spent our first Christmas with our mattresses on the living room floor. It was fun, frustrating, terrifying, and exhilarating all at the same time.

There were little things then that reflect our journey today. Like our Christmas tree. I was so frustrated with construction dust that I purchased a flocked tree, which we still own. It's a beautiful reminder of our journey and the hard work we put into bringing a vision to life. Over time, we built a life we're proud to pass on to our children.

Around that time, I began practicing daily gratitude. I focused on the things that were going right, projects coming to fruition, a newly budded herb or vegetable. The whole experience settled my restless spirit.

It would take us three hard years of work to complete the interior of the home. These days, I like to think the work will never be done—we still have to build a shop, expand our goat housing, build a bocce ball court, expand the garden, and so much more. I learned to drive a Bobcat, built a pond, and mastered a jackhammer during the demolition phase of the old front porch. And from those moments, I realized that the journey is the sweetest part of it all. In a world of BEFOREs and AFTERs, the DURINGs are pretty fantastic.

Finding Professional Fulfillment

My newfound personal growth and fulfillment highlighted my lack of professional fulfillment. I had ignited a spark by living a servant-focused life. I was giving back, gardening, building a farm, raising animals, and teaching my girls the definition of hard work. But my work life still required the same attention.

Just like my former, perfectly fine cul-de-sac life, I had a perfectly fine job and a career history that was steady and looked amazing on paper. I came into staffing and recruiting haphazardly, the way so many of us do. I had just finished school in Utah when my Mima (my southern grandmother who'd raised me since the time I was 12) said, "Why don't you become a Kelly Girl?" So, I signed up and ended up with a job at a pharmaceutical company working on trends and analysis. One pay week cycle, they forgot to pay me. Later, the Kelly Sales Representative, Debbie, dropped my check off to me in person (apparently this was a big account). We started a conversation and became fast friends. When the pharmaceutical company I was temping for was purchased, Debbie approached me about working directly for Kelly as a recruiter. I said yes, and the rest is history!

I've had many supervisors over the course of my career, but very few true leaders. Growing up in the industry, there were limited opportunities for women. It was a strange game navigating the twists and turns of workplace relationships with other females. I found out early (and the hard way) that not every woman is there to support you or has your best interests at heart. Still, my career took off quickly, and I was offered leadership opportunities early. I faced significant challenges as a young female leader and often found myself justifying many of my decisions and my worthiness, silencing any needs I had to avoid showing signs of weakness. I took what was given and didn't complain.

> " *I promised myself I would not shy away from opportunities or conversations in the future. I would no longer accept having career regrets. I was going to act and take risks.* "

The year my youngest daughter was born was also the year that "How Fast Can You Return to Work?" badges were being proudly (and metaphorically) worn by women. Obviously, with my comparison issues, I was not to be outdone. I took only five weeks off, express pumped in the middle of conference calls, and raced to the sitter during lunch to feed my baby. Certainly not ideal, and something I now know many women have struggled with in their work life.

As my career continued and I gruelingly climbed the corporate ladder at large enterprise firms, a continuing theme I noticed was the total lack of female support or comradery. It was a bloody competition, and only the most masculine women survived. I was never any good at being anyone other than myself, so I stunk at corporate politics. My first experience at being laid off would afford me the opportunity to go smaller and work for a local firm that was right in my backyard.

It was bizarre going from a large enterprise employer to a small, locally-owned shop. But the change was welcome because I had employers who appreciated me and gave me autonomy, flexibility to work from home, and plenty of support. And yet, as my personal life came into focus, it became obvious that I was still searching for something in my professional life. I was grappling with the "Why?" of it all. Frankly, I think my employer at that time was paying for the sins of past employers and experiences.

As far back as I can remember, I've been defined by my work in a very unhealthy way. I would assign personal value to what I achieved at work and how my latest boss evaluated me. I found myself particularly wounded by the judgmental or spiteful words of female co-workers. What I failed to recognize was that evaluations, feedback, and reviews were almost always filled with bias. They should not have reflected who I was (or am) as a human being. Unfortunately, we usually don't see things with such clarity in the moment. The process becomes even more painful when those delivering the information don't have your best interests at heart.

Reflecting on my career helped me shape my work priorities. One of those priorities was what I called: "No what ifs." I promised myself I would not shy away from opportunities or conversations in the future. I would no longer accept having career regrets. I was going to act and take risks. I looked back on past outcomes, steadfast in my belief that—while there were unfortunate leaders and some terrible behavior—I was still responsible for those outcomes. I knew I had the strength to change those outcomes in the future. And I was just beginning to find my voice.

Consider All Your Options

My dad has always said, "Every conversation is a conversation worth having." In the moment, it seemed so hard, like such a betrayal to explore new professional options. I was wrought with guilt. I was perfectly happy and perfectly valued at the small local agency—so, *why* was I considering other options? Because I didn't want to live with any regrets. During my time of personal growth, I promised myself never to let *me* down again.

So, I had a conversation that resulted in an opportunity, which then turned into an offer to return to a large enterprise firm. I simply couldn't say no. Did the risk end up in reward? In short, yes, it did. Had, I not taken that opportunity, I would not be where I am today. Literally, had I stayed at my "perfectly fine" job at the local firm, the outcome would have been very different when the pandemic hit. Instead, I was able to accomplish some amazing things on a global level, gain some experience I didn't have, and learn things I hadn't previously known.

Then, without warning, I walked into an office and saw the Head of Human Resources sitting there. I'll admit, it was tough. I don't care how it's phrased—laid off, fired, reduced, furloughed—it all feels like rejection. No matter what I told myself, my confidence was still rocked. It felt like a punch to the gut. I had taken the risk, committed to my mantra of no "what ifs," and still been burned.

I had failed.

Why You SHOULD Do This

Suddenly, the choice to do things on my own terms was removed. That little fire in my belly—which was just a thought while I was gainfully employed—was more important than ever to execute on. While I plotted my business ideas, I also responsibly engaged in traditional interviews. But as the pandemic grew bleaker, so did potential job opportunities.

Leap Consulting Solutions has its own origin story that stems from the relationship I share with my husband. It also has a special meaning as an acronym. You see, I'm a "Sally Safety" type, and he's more of a "build your wings on the way down" kind of guy. When I told him I was thinking of starting my own business, he told me to "take the leap!" Then, an additional idea popped into my head. The acronym "L.E.A.P" represented our family. It stands for Lauren, Emily, Allison, and Peter—myself, my two girls, and my husband. It was only fitting that my new business represent the sentiment and the WHY behind my actions: my family.

I wasn't quite sure what my business would be, but I knew I was good at a few things and that I was great at helping businesses grow in a healthy way. So, I subscribed to the KISS thought process (Keep It Simple Silly), and I set out to nail down the three ways I could make a positive impact on a business. At Leap, we help organizations build technical solutions relevant to their organization, improve the way they do business, and guide them through the change. We call this process "Define, Develop, Deliver." That simplicity is what has helped my firm achieve significant growth in just two short years and solidify my brand in the industry. If there was a singular piece of advice I would give any new business owner, it would be to keep your offerings simple.

Now, my goal is to pay it forward to every female entrepreneur I meet by sharing my story and what I learned.

While preparing to write this chapter, I looked at my journals and all the thoughts I'd jotted down when I had been having an internal battle with myself. "Do I, or don't I?" was a constant question I asked. Below are the notes I wrote:

Why you shouldn't do this:

- "I'm 46—way too old to start something like this."
- "We need medical benefits."

- "What's your value proposition? Do you know enough about staffing?"
- "You've never owned your own business."
- "Who will buy from me?"

I read those words now, and they sort of hurt my soul. I wish I could tell that former version of myself that everything would be okay. I have now rewritten that terrible list of negative self-talk for every woman reading this who has an idea, or a spark, or a teeny tiny vision of doing it on her own. Here is my new, more appropriate list:

Why you SHOULD do this:

- "46 is just getting started."
- "Buy your own benefits—it's 2021."
- "Pick three things. Start there, memorize them, and tell everyone who will listen."
- "I've actually run VERY successful businesses, just not with my own money—so the talent is there. This time, there's just more skin in the game."
- "If you believe it, your buyers will come."

After all my years struggling with women in the workforce, taking the time to surround myself with the right women paid off. Can you guess who showed up for me first? Yup, women. Specifically, the Lady Leaders you'll read more about in this book. They extended their hands to me and helped me rise. Now, we continue to do that for others. We pay it forward today, and we'll continue to do so in the future. We figured out quickly that when the tough got going, women took action.

Opening your own business is not for the faint of heart. I wake up excited and terrified every day. But each day, month, and year brings new challenges, changes, and opportunities to tackle. I've realized a few things:

- Everyone has to start somewhere.
- All experts start out as beginners.
- If you're afraid to suck at something for a little bit, you'll never get started.
- Starting is the hardest part.
- Keep it simple.
- "Done is better than perfect, always." This translates to: You can analyze all day long; but in the end, action speaks much louder than perfection. (Thanks to Heather Monahan for that piece of advice.)

I share these valuable lessons to help you see a path forward. During the pandemic, I was able to replace my corporate income, sell my first million-dollar account, and close my first partnership. In my first year, I increased my followership on LinkedIn from 5k to over 20K. I also solidified a co-host spot on a top industry podcast. And most importantly, I found a group of women who will support me through thick and thin. Year two of Leap has been more of the same, only better. We tripled sales, added nearly another 20k in followers, and added a number of new accolades to our resume. And most importantly, I've done everything I can to pay it forward and stay grounded in gratitude.

Your tribe is an essential part of your ability to grow. Choose them wisely. When you find them, never let go, and never take them for granted.

Lauren B. Jones

Lauren B. Jones (also known as LJ) has been a leader, influencer, and innovator in the staffing industry for over 24 years. Lauren's obsession with technology has helped shape her career, as she's built an esteemed reputation as a tech stack expert, industry trailblazer, and business operations guru. She founded Leap Consulting Solutions with the intent of supporting businesses and adding clarity to the steps required to digitally transform with excellence.

Lauren has been named to the list of Top 15 Staffing Professionals to watch for in 2021, as well as the Power List of Top 200 Thought Influencers to watch in 2021. She's been featured on almost every industry podcast, including *Settle Smarter*, *You Own the Experience Podcast* (which she now co-hosts), *Ivy Podcast*, *Staffing Hub*, *HR Lift Off*, and more. On these podcasts, she passionately shares her knowledge of technology. Her LinkedIn vlog has grown her following with popular hashtag days like #technologytuesday and #womencrushwednesday.

Lauren is active in her community, supporting organizations like NCL, Women's Empowerment, Saint John's Program, and more. Lauren is a recent empty nester and proud mom to two powerhouse boss ladies, Emily and Allison. Lauren lives on a farm in Elk Grove, California with her husband, Peter.

https://www.linkedin.com/in/goatleader/
lauren@leapconsultingsolutions.com

SINK TO SWIM

Janette Marx

The storm had passed.
Yet Poseidon and Neptune appeared to be fighting
for control of the ocean.
The waves were terrifying.
The boats looked like they would capsize.
Who would ever scuba dive in these conditions?
Me.

Since I love a good challenge and was celebrating my 20-year wedding anniversary, I wanted to enjoy a dive. We set out and immediately felt the anger of the ocean. We were tossed from side to side in the dive boat. When we reached the point in the ocean where we were going to dive, our dive master instructed us all to jump in carefully, one by one, and immediately descend to a safe distance to wait for the rest of the dive party. It was not safe on the surface.

I descended immediately after jumping in. As I sank, I felt the calm waters of the ocean. I descended slowly, equalizing the pressure in my ears, and found my way to the proper depth needed to achieve "neutral buoyancy." That's the point where you aren't sinking anymore, and you aren't floating back up to the surface; you exist in the water perfectly still and calm. During that moment, I started to feel the peace and change around me. The rough waters were high above, on the surface. Once everyone had reached this depth, we moved forward with small kicks in our desired direction. We were able to enjoy the surroundings of the ocean.

I find challenges throughout life are like this. When you are on the surface of a challenge and fight against it, you're in a position where you risk drowning. But if you dive down, embrace the "sink," and begin to understand the depth and reality of the issue, you can find acceptance in the water—your neutral buoyancy. Only then can you deal with the constant pressure and find your way forward.

Leadership is a compilation of several learned skills, much like diving. And the best lessons are often taught through real life experiences and recognizing how we respond to circumstances. Our experiences shape us into who we are as people and leaders. One of the foundational elements that shaped my career and leadership style is resilience; without it, I would not be the leader I am today.

Challenges make life interesting. Sometimes, we seek challenges— other times, they find us. Our level of resilience is sharpened with each challenge we overcome. To have resilience, one must be able to communicate with intention, have the courage to confront reality, possess the ability to navigate certain situations under pressure, and know how to adapt in order to thrive in life. Things don't simply happen to you; it is your response that sets you apart. Your responses to challenges are completely in your control.

There are many early life experiences that could have sunk me. Instead, they shaped the leader I am today, sharpened my resiliency, and taught me how to sink to swim.

Communicate Intentionally – Or Be Eaten Alive!

Since you can't speak when you're underwater, communication comes by way of hand signals, facial expressions, touch, and alternative sounds. On a separate occasion diving with my husband, we were in the back of the dive group when a large shark began encircling us. My husband grabbed my leg, then pointed forward to make sure I saw the shark. As we watched the shark, he thought, "If the shark attacks, the person in the back of the group will get eaten." So, he wanted us safely established in the front. He communicated that with good intent, yet I did not fully understand him. Once he had reached the front of the group, he looked back at me. Now I was the one who would be eaten alive! I understood half the message, not the whole thing. It reminded me of an experience I'd had in middle school.

The first time I really had this sinking feeling came the summer before seventh grade. That was when I found out how mean girls can be. That summer, one of my friends called me and started talking negatively about our other friends. I was a young girl who didn't like confrontation, so I listened and went along with the conversation. When I went to school on the first day of seventh grade, I found out my whole group of friends was mad at me. I soon discovered that another girl had been on that call silently listening to us. She told everyone that I was speaking badly about them. In that world, my silence meant agreement, rather than just trying to avoid confrontation. After that, I learned quickly that you need to find your voice and speak up. Otherwise, people will speak for you. As a result, I found a new group of friends. They became my closest confidants for years to come.

Those seventh-grade girls ate me alive due to my lack of clear, direct communication—luckily, the shark didn't! People communicate in unique ways and receive information differently. One must understand their audience and adapt their style to ensure their message is being received. To build resilience, one must communicate with intention to be properly understood.

Confront Reality – Don't Let it Sink You!

One of those new friends helped me with my next sinking moment in life. When I entered my freshman year of high school, I felt like I had it all—the perfect family, community, and a school full of activities. On October 25th, 1989, that all changed. My parents informed me they were getting divorced. Despair, surprise, and shock took hold of me. My life was changing, and I couldn't stop it. At that point in time, the divorce rate per 1,000 in the population was 4.7. It was not common amongst my friends. The news shook me and my three sisters. Our foundation and personal security were disrupted. The four of us would stay in our family home with our father. I needed to accept the situation and confront my new reality.

The sinking feeling was real. I was falling deep into the water— where no one should swim. With diving, if you go too deep, the pressure of the water will wreak havoc on your ears and body, which is why neutral buoyancy is crucial. In life, finding a neutral state— where you can accept a situation, deal with it with a balanced perspective, and then move forward—is critical. This realization hit me the day the moving truck pulled up to the house. I felt myself sinking too deep. In tears, I ran a mile to my friend's house (yes, one of the new friends I'd made in the seventh grade), and she helped me through my pain. Finding a good friend, an ally, helps you achieve neutral buoyancy faster. It ensures you don't sink to the depths of the ocean.

I needed to find myself before I could help my sisters. I played the role of peacemaker in the family. In doing so, I found I was able to learn foundational leadership skills in our home. I learned how to problem solve, multi-task, and prioritize what was most important in life. Through these experiences, I learned how to take care of others' emotional and physical well-being. My emotional intelligence was tested and strengthened.

As a leader, you need to find your own strength before you can lend it to others. Sometimes, those occurrences happen simultaneously. Pressure is constant while working through a challenge. Learning to regulate the pressure, accept it, and work through it is key to forward progress.

Own the Outcome – Navigate Through the Dark!

I recently had the opportunity to go cave diving. This is a unique experience, especially considering one can feel constrained or trapped in a cave. With cave diving, you must stay calm to find your path. If you panic, you can't rush to the surface for a breath of air (which you should never do anyway) because the cave surrounds you! We swam with flashlights to see through the dark parts of the cave. There are moments when you can't tell which way is up, down, left, or right. You must follow the directional lines to navigate your way through.

My high school sweetheart and I experienced that sinking feeling—as if we were in our own cave—when we found out we were pregnant. I was only 19. We felt surrounded by darkness, not knowing which direction to go. We were on our own. We could barely make our monthly rent, and we knew living like that wasn't sustainable. Panicking wasn't an option; figuring out our situation and moving forward, together, was our only way out. We needed to create a way forward for ourselves and our future family. So, instead of giving up on my future career and education, we created a plan.

Our plan was simple. We would each support the other through college. I would work first while my husband went to school and played collegiate basketball. Once he graduated, I would resign, go to school full-time, and he would support the family. The result of this meant that I started my career very early. I entered the recruitment industry and fell in love with it. And I excelled, getting promotions for my performance every six months for four years straight. Suddenly, I didn't want to do anything else. I enjoyed putting people to work and taking care of companies who needed great talent. When my husband graduated and got his first job out of college, I was so far along in my career that it would've been foolish to resign. I shifted my plan, and he supported me while I finished my degree at night. I was still working a full-time job.

Juggling our family life wasn't easy, but it made us better people in the long run.

Through this experience, I embraced the blessing life provided us. My pregnancy turned into the best thing that ever happened to either of us. Our son is the only child we were blessed with, and I'm so happy we have him. I wouldn't change a thing about our experience, as it taught me perseverance, focus, and drive. It lit a fire in me that can't be extinguished. My internal flame—this drive to be successful in the workforce and support my family so we'd never feel in the dark again—created the momentum that drove so many parts of my success.

Sometimes in life, you might experience what *seems* like a big setback. But if you own the outcome and deal with it head on, difficult moments can become extremely rewarding. The journey may not be exactly what you had imagined, but it's still beautiful. You can have expectations when you're diving, but you can't control what any specific dive will bring. This may not have been the path I wanted since day one—but navigating life's twists and turns strengthened my ability to be agile and open. And that has led me to what I have today.

I ultimately earned my MBA from Duke University's Fuqua School of Business when I was 34. I became a CEO at 43. I was always the youngest to hold each leadership role throughout my career. I didn't stop when life got dark—I kept moving forward.

Adapt to Thrive – Don't Drown in the Waves of Adversity

The first five years of my career were full of growing and excelling alongside different leaders I had the pleasure of learning from. I had a thirst for constant improvement, and I soaked up all their knowledge. I was reporting to a leader whom I respected greatly. But then my world turned upside down when our company completed a major acquisition. As a result, territory lines were redrawn, and so was the organizational structure. I had a new boss.

I meant to accept the change and do my best to be helpful to my new group of colleagues. I tried to assist them with insights into our processes, terminology, and systems. What I didn't realize was that the help wasn't wanted from my direct supervisor, which created a strained relationship. It only continued to deteriorate over time.

I felt lost. I realized I wasn't working for someone who had my best interests at heart when she told me, in such a way as to put me in my place and deflate me: "It took me nine years to become a VP; it will take you at least that long." I was stagnating, working for someone who wanted me gone.

The negativity also started to affect my team. I was leading an office of 15 people, and we had been doing well before the acquisition. But before my eyes, I saw the divisiveness and how it was destroying what we had. She tried to get my SVP to fire me over trivial reasons, but she didn't have the backing to fire me because of my past performance. We weren't working well together, and I suddenly didn't want to perform anymore. It got to the point that I was intentionally not doing well because I didn't want to make her look good. I was adding to the problem, and I needed change.

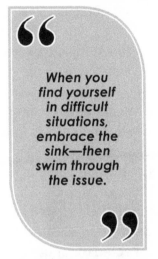

When you find yourself in difficult situations, embrace the sink—then swim through the issue.

I had to decide: do I stay or leave? If I stayed, I needed to change. I had to accept the situation and find a way forward for us to work together. Many would have left and started anew. But I decided to stay and change. The situation was dire, and I had to create a better environment for myself and my team. During the next four months, we started building the business and culture back. It wasn't easy, but I was determined. And I knew that with focus, a positive attitude, and better understanding, we could navigate the situation.

Suddenly, I received a call and was told that she'd resigned. It felt like the pressure of the entire ocean had been lifted off me. My team also noticed, and we took off swimming again. In the last six months of that year, our turnaround was so powerful that we reached the top five percent of performing offices for the company. We even received recognition for Branch of the Year (out of 100 eligible branches) the following year. Our turnaround was spectacular.

Enduring this experience and working through it instead of giving up resulted in an opportunity to shine. I gained loyalty from other leaders in the company for sticking with a tough situation. My next leader understood my capabilities and supported my growth and development. This leader promoted me to VP when I was 26! It didn't take nine years, it took two. By 30, I was moving to the East Coast to be a Senior Vice President.

Rough waters shaped me. I wasn't diving; I was trying to swim on the surface amongst the waves, and I was drowning. Once I accepted the situation and fully sank into it and let it surround me, I was able to find my neutral buoyancy and safely swim forward. Utilize your network and your personal board of directors. Lean on your allies to help you through difficult situations. Above all else, know that you have the power to adapt to situations and change outcomes. The power is always within yourself to thrive.

Keep Swimming

Everyone has a peaceful place where you can think, assess, and feel calm. For me, it's always been in the water. When you are confronted with challenges, it's important to find your peaceful place. This place should allow you to confront your situation head on and discover your way forward. That's how people become resilient.

When you find yourself in difficult situations, embrace the sink— *then* swim through the issue. I have found it helpful to first sink into the situation and let it fully surround me. By removing myself from the dangerous waters and descending into the depth of the issue, I can better understand it. This helps me to communicate clearly and with intention. Once someone understands the issue, they will have the proper insight to confront reality. From there, a plan can be created. Owning the outcome is key to staying calm, keeping your mental state clear, and reorienting yourself so you can then swim through the issue. Confidence increases with the ability to adapt successfully to any challenge, and the swim becomes much more pleasant. Success is about forward progress. Move forward and enjoy the scenery along the way! In the end, you'll appreciate the peace that comes with it, and you will thrive in business and in life.

When you are finished with a dive and start to ascend, before you get to the surface, you conduct a "Safety Stop" at 15 feet. This stop allows your body and lungs to reorient themselves to the level of pressure you've been under. After five minutes, you can then safely return to surface. As you surface from a challenge, use a Safety Stop to reorient yourself, collect your thoughts, remove the pressure, and push forward.

As leaders, we face challenges daily. It's important to take care of yourself mentally and physically before you can care for others. Leaders are constantly being watched by others and looked to for guidance. So, realize the impact you make on others, find your strength in resiliency, and lead the way forward by *embracing the SINK.*

Janette Marx

Janette Marx is the CEO of Airswift, a billion-dollar global workforce solutions company focused in energy, process, and infrastructure industries. Marx first joined the company as COO in 2014. In 2016, she led the integration of Swift Worldwide Resources and Air Energi, who merged to form Airswift. The 25-year industry veteran recently led a groundbreaking merger with Competentia, thus establishing Airswift as the world's foremost provider of technical workforce solutions.

Marx is involved in several different community and philanthropic activities including the American Cancer Society's CEOs Against Cancer, Junior Achievement, American Staffing Association, University of Houston's Bauer School of Business, and the Greater Houston Women's Chamber of Commerce. She is a champion of building people's careers and serves as an Ambassador for Equity in Energy for the US Department of Energy.

Marx is featured on Staffing Industry Analysts' Staffing 100 in North America list and the Global Power 150 Women in Staffing list. She was also recognized as an energy industry leader in the Houston Business Journal's Women Who Mean Business, named as a "Breakthrough Woman" by the Greater Houston Women's Chamber of Commerce, and received the Leader of Influence award from the World Affairs Council. Marx earned an MBA from Duke's Fuqua School of Business and holds a bachelor's degree in business management.

Janette enjoys spending time with her husband, son, and dog at their family home in Houston. They enjoy traveling, music, sports, and the outdoors. Family vacations are frequent, preferably to a spot with unique diving opportunities! Janette loves spending time with her extended family, including her parents, three sisters, three stepsisters, two sisters-in-law, eight brothers-in-law, and twenty-seven nieces and nephews!

https://www.linkedin.com/in/janettemarx/
janettemarx@gmail.com

PUTTING HAPPINESS TO WORK

Robin Mee

C an happiness be a goal? For me, the answer is yes. Happiness has been my #1 goal for as long as I can remember. I was always rather embarrassed by simply wanting to be happy. Other people's goals seemed far loftier, while wanting to be happy sounded rather simple. But in recent years, happiness has become a cultural phenomenon. It's huge. Universities have courses on happiness. Yale's happiness class is online and free. Harvard has been conducting a study on happiness that started in the 1930's. There are tons of books, articles, podcasts, quizzes, and TED Talks about happiness. Go search "happiness" on Google—millions of results will pop up.

The pursuit of happiness is my north star. It is the pillar upon which I have built my life, and it serves as the perspective that frames my world experiences. When I am happy, I am my best self. Being happy is one of the most important choices I make every day. It is my priority. Every decision is mapped against my happiness barometer. Smiling sets the tone. Framing conversations from a positive perspective communicates intention.

I think everyone can be happy, regardless of their situation in life and despite personal history. I am struck by how few prioritize happiness. I think some people might be embarrassed by the concept or see it as a weakness.

I'm fortunate to be born in America, where we pride ourselves on opportunity for all. Where education is free, and the myth of Horatio Alger—that everyone can achieve wealth and success through hard work—is alive and well. I believe in working hard, and that we make our own luck. You've likely heard the saying, "The harder I work, the luckier I get." I believe in that philosophy, but there are plenty of things outside of our control.

Some of us were more fortunate than others with the families we were born into. My husband had a stable and traditional upbringing with two loving parents, four close siblings, and financial security. My family was fractured by alcoholism, yet my mother rose up in the face of adversity. She loved me and my siblings unconditionally and created a safe, comfortable home for us. She provided stability and achieved success as a civil rights and women's rights advocate. I overcame many challenges and learned lots of lessons during my first 18 years of life, all of which shaped my worldview.

I'm a natural-born optimist, but you don't have to be an optimist to aspire to happiness. When happiness is at the center of your decision making, everything seems brighter. Fully aware of challenges, conflict, and negativity, I choose to focus on what aligns with my values. Sometimes I stumble, make the wrong choice, or make no decision at all. Like everyone, I deal with daily adversity. But I try to frame challenges from a positive perspective and take time to thoughtfully respond before reacting.

In no particular order, here is a short list of things essential to my happiness:

Achieving Balance: I seek equilibrium. Personal and professional balance requires self-awareness and regular readjustments. From an early age, I knew I wanted to have a family. I also wanted a career and open-ended financial opportunities. Seeing my mom support our family showed me the importance of being self-reliant. But she did not strive for balance. She was a workaholic and a gambler later in life—an all-or-nothing kind of person. From watching her, I learned what I wanted but also what I didn't want. My perspective of balance changes over time but keeps me in a zone that provides context to my decision making. For example, once during a stressful time of our lives, my son shared with me that—despite the 24/7 demands of my being an entrepreneur and the fact that I was always working—he knew I always put our family first. I knew from his comment that I was successfully balancing work in a way that emotionally supported my family, which was most important to me. That puts a smile on my face to this day.

Connection: Connecting people is my superpower. I always put relationships first, and I have a large network of friends and acquaintances, both in business and personally. Family is my number one priority, and they know it. But my close friends are my extended family, and they also know how important they are to me. Is it coincidental or purposeful that I found a career where I connect people for a living? How great is it that I continue to make meaningful connections with new people daily in my work?

A Quest for Knowledge: Intellectual stimulation. Always being curious. I consider myself a life-long learner and read daily for pleasure and business. I like to surround myself with people and opportunities from which to expand my knowledge. That often means stretching outside of my comfort zone and doing things that I am not experienced in or naturally inclined to do, like public speaking. Anyone who knows me knows that I ask a lot of questions, and that I'm a thoughtful listener.

Being Outdoors: Sunsets and sunrises. The sky. Being near water. The changing seasons. As an adult, I realized how important the natural world is to me. Twenty years ago, I moved to my current home, which is surrounded by old growth trees, lots of wildlife, and is a five-minute walk to a national park and the Potomac River. I appreciate being outside every day. Daily dog walks provide structured outdoor time. I have become a gardener with a growing understanding and appreciation of plants. Enjoying nature has a meditative quality that is enhanced by being present in the moment. COVID provided an opportunity to spend more time than ever outside in all kinds of weather, and it was fun wrapping up in blankets around a fire pit with family and friends—even if it was 35 degrees!

Adventuring and Exploring New Terrain: Be it a new restaurant, a walking path, or simply a drive down a road I've never been on before. It could be a new book or a new acquaintance. I am energized by new experiences and intentionally create as many as possible.

Health: I make it a priority to eat nourishing, organic, locally grown food. Who doesn't like shopping at local farmers markets? My husband and I like to cook at home where we can control quality and quantities. I stay active, drink massive amounts of filtered water, sleep well, get annual medical check-ups, and stay up to date with vaccines and CDC guidance. Being healthy is super important to me.

Giving: Unconditional generosity—both professionally and personally with no strings attached—makes me feel good. Volunteering, making charitable contributions, or providing counsel to others are some examples. At my company, we created a program called **MeeDerby Gives Thanks**. With this fund, we make annual donations in the names of our clients and industry partners to the charities of their choice. 35 years ago, our family "adopted" and helped another family in need, and to this day we remain deeply connected. I have lots of conversations with people who just need to talk, and I aim to provide as much support to them as I can. I enjoy mentoring, in my company, and through the American Staffing Association (ASA). It feels great to give with an open heart and expect nothing in return.

Making Others Happy: Does that sound silly? I'm not a pushover, and I negotiate daily in my work, but I strive to meet people in the middle. I'm a huge fan of Maya Angelou's quote, "I've learned that people will forget what you said, people will forget what you did, but people will never forget how you made them feel." I know I can't "make" someone happy, and that the feeling must come from within them. But I do hope to influence people positively in every interaction.

Communicating Honestly, Thoughtfully, and Directly: I try to listen actively and with empathy. Set appropriate expectations. Provide compassionate feedback. These traits are at the center of who I strive to be.

The Need for Security: Growing up in my family was sometimes rocky, but as an adult I've made solid decisions that have created stability in my life. Planning for the future has grounded my life in a way that gives me control, order, and comfort. Creating and contributing annually to a profit-sharing plan for my employees is an example of this. In doing so, I know I am helping my team save for retirement and support their families' long-term financial goals.

Always Having Something to Look Forward To: Making plans, which usually involves traveling or getting together with family and friends, are high on my list. Having something to look forward to keeps me excited, engaged, and looking positively towards the future. Some might say that I plan too much. While that is true, I am flexible to shift as necessary. There is much that I want to accomplish, and planning helps create my roadmap. I appreciate new opportunities regularly coming my way, and I try to say yes as often as possible even when it takes me out of my comfort zone (like writing this essay). Although I love to read, writing does not come easily or naturally to me. I can be a great procrastinator, and I know I must carve out quiet, uninterrupted time to think and write.

Limiting Exposure to Negativity: I purposefully monitor my consumption of news and social media. I generally tune out negativity as it brings me down and sits heavy on my psyche. That includes people, television, and a whole host of other things.

Desire For Control: I have always wanted to be in control of my own destiny. It was definitely one of the factors in starting my own business. I'm collaborative and love working with others, but I hate being told what to do. Having a voice and being heard is critical to my well-being. The power to make my own decisions and maintain the personal power of influence, while staying open and flexible, is central to my happiness.

How Do These Traits Fit Into My Professional Choices?

There is deep satisfaction in putting people to work. In 1988, I founded (and now lead) a small business called MeeDerby, an executive search firm that specializes in the staffing industry and workforce solutions ecosystem. We impact the lives of so many by helping them find happiness in their work and elevating their careers, ultimately providing financial benefits that sustain individuals, families, and future generations. Having a stable and fulfilling job is a basic need, as it supports all the other critical basic necessities of life. Everything comes full circle when the staffing professionals we've placed in other staffing companies go on to impact the lives of people they're now responsible for serving.

> " The power to make my own decisions and maintain the personal power of influence, while staying open and flexible, is central to my happiness. "

I am incredibly fortunate to have been empowered to start my own business. Finding work that aligns with my core values and natural attributes has been a true joy of my life. I enjoy being my own boss, although I have many people whom I support, collaborate with, and "report" to. For 33 years at MeeDerby, I've been surrounded by an incredible team of people—a solid core of like-minded professionals who embrace the same values of community, communication, integrity, and results. These people are passionate about the staffing industry and have been with MeeDerby for a long time. Our average tenure is over 17 years, which I consider a strong indicator of people being happy in their jobs. I appreciate our team of staffing subject matter experts—their advice and perspective are highly regarded.

MeeDerby was a relative pioneer in hiring and managing a remote team. In 2010, the company evolved from having a Washington, D.C. corporate headquarters (on K Street, around the corner from the White House) to remote officing with staff across the country. This was years before the COVID pandemic sent many Americans home to work.

As our business became national in scope, we recognized that a remote team could be empowered to perform at high levels of productivity while still maintaining flexibility to support families and outside interests, which can be more difficult to manage with grueling commutes and travel schedules. We aspire to innovate and harness technology in a way that allows us to work effectively. Technology provides us access to people, to each other, and enhances individual work-life balance. It also provides everyone the power to work from anywhere, which creates such a sense of freedom when compared to being tethered to a desk or traditional office.

I am passionate about MeeDerby's mission. There is great satisfaction in helping people find great jobs and elevate their careers, and helping companies identify hidden talent. We make a difference in the lives of the people and industry we serve.

Volunteering and giving back to the staffing industry also gives me great satisfaction. My first boss in the staffing industry was Peter Yesnee, who went on to start Staffing Industry Analysts (SIA), the leading global advisor on staffing and workforce solutions. One of Peter's favorite quotes, originally from John Key, was "You get out of life what you put in." I took that advice to heart. When I started MeeDerby, I sought a community of staffing professionals, and I selfishly wanted to be part of something bigger than myself. Getting involved with ASA as a volunteer provided the outlet I sought. I've held dozens of volunteer leadership roles at ASA, both locally in the DC metro area where I reside and on a national level. MeeDerby is currently a sponsor of the Women in Leadership Interest Group, which I helped co-found within ASA. The work of helping women rise up, along with getting involved with Diversity, Equity, and Inclusion (DE&I), are current initiatives that deeply resonate with me. Along with ASA, SIA, and the Women's Business Collaborative (WBC), this community has provided public forums for me to give back by contributing my time and expertise in meaningful ways. After all, I am my mother's daughter.

I'm wrapping up this project with a smile on my face and a sense of satisfaction. Being part of the Lady Leader Book Club—the 15 women who are writing this book—is a silver lining born of the COVID pandemic. A group of us were planning a dinner in mid-March of 2020 to celebrate Joyce Russell and the publication of her first book, *Put a Cherry on Top*. Our dinner morphed into a Zoom meeting, which became a monthly forum where we read a book and had the author present to our group. Along the way we have made new friends, deepened existing relationships, participated in a Zoom cooking class, met a world-renowned fashion designer, launched a DE&I subgroup, conducted business together, and wrote this book. We've shared experiences, supported each other, laughed, cried, and laughed some more. Most importantly, we are contributing to a long-overdue movement focused on elevating women and diversity in the Staffing Industry. The Lady Leaders Book Club coalesced under the leadership of Lauren Jones and Leslie Vickrey, two amazing women with extraordinary energy, passion, and intelligence. Since then, the club has taken on a life of its own.

Am I happy all the time? Absolutely not. There are many things that I want and need to be more intentional about. Do I have regrets? Sure, just like everyone else, although really not many. Do I have daily challenges that I must choose how to respond to? Absolutely, but I own the choices I make, strive to show up daily as my authentic self, and am excited about what the future holds.

Robin Mee

Robin Mee is the Founder and President of MeeDerby, the leading search firm for the Workforce Solutions ecosystem. She is a passionate advocate of staffing, a volunteer industry leader, and a regular speaker at staffing events nationally.

Staffing Industry Analysts (SIA) has honored Robin many times on the Staffing 100 and Global Women's Power 150 lists. The American Staffing Association (ASA) recognized Robin with their inaugural Volunteer of the Year Award. Robin is a vocal supporter of Women in Leadership as well as issues of Diversity and Inclusion, and MeeDerby is a supporting sponsor of the ASA's Women in Leadership Interest Group. Staffing companies have voted MeeDerby a Best of Staffing firm 11 times for client satisfaction in the annual ClearlyRated survey.

Most importantly, Robin and her team at MeeDerby are highly regarded members of the staffing community whose company is a conduit for change. MeeDerby has helped hundreds of staffing companies grow by hiring top talent, and thousands of staffing professionals elevate their careers.

https://www.linkedin.com/in/robinmee/
robin@meederby.com
301-263-2663x1

THE OUTSIDE LOOKING IN

Kimberly Pope

F rom the outside looking in, my childhood in Columbus, Ohio was perfect. I had all the community support a kid needed to grow, a great school system, supportive friends, and a safe neighborhood where people often left their doors unlocked. In the summers, my friends and I would ride our bikes to a local, 50s-style diner and order shakes and fries. We would chat about whatever VHS tape we had watched the night before. After eating lunch, we would cross the street to spend the afternoon at the community pool. Rain or shine, we laughed and played with no care in the world for anything other than those moments.

But when the sun started to set and my friends gathered their things to head home, my carefree attitude would turn to one of dread as I hopped on my bike to ride home.

When I entered my house, it was as if the best days would end in a second. My parents constantly fought with each other about money or taking care of my baby sister and brother. They yelled from across the house, and I often found myself trying to intervene. As the oldest child, the burden of this responsibility was placed on me. And because I was older, my parents expected me to look after myself.

My parents hardly noticed when I was gone, off staying with friends to get to and from school. Even more insidious was the lack of emotional safety I felt with them. When I would tell them about my hopes and dreams for the future, they consistently told me I would not be able to achieve what I sought, that I could not afford to get there. When my interventions in their fights turned into long-fought battles with my mom, my dad would tell me to focus on myself. "The only person you can change is yourself," he'd say.

I thought long and hard about this statement during my early years. It was something that I did not realize until more recently and, after becoming a mother, it has defined how I make all my decisions. But at first, it was something that I took to heart, as I spent time reading self-help books and looking inward to improve myself. I believed that if I did take his advice and focus on myself, I would eventually be happy.

I felt so alone in my house as a child, but I was grateful for the community. They saw what I was going through and offered support. My friends and their parents became family, and they helped me see what I needed to do to get out of that situation. I slowly realized that my community was helping to change and influence me to help build up my confidence. By my senior year of high school, after years of balancing schoolwork with part-time jobs and competitive training in field hockey, I had earned my ticket out: an athletic scholarship to Appalachian State University in Boone, North Carolina. I had no idea how I was going to make it work, but I was determined to leave.

When Your True Self Emerges

In college, I focused on survival. Without any financial support from my parents to pay for college, I worked three jobs simultaneously while studying and attending daily field hockey practices. I learned the art of bouncing checks, living off microwaveable noodles, and building relationships with friends who became family. At my lowest, I even resorted to paying tuition with a credit card. But during this time, I understood what it felt like to ask for help, to lean on people who cared about me. This experience gave me a sense of hope for what my adult life had to come.

From these low moments, I felt my true self emerge. Through life-long relationships with my teammates and strong time management skills gained out of necessity, I began to see how the foundation of my career journey was being built. Being a Division One athlete gave me the confidence I needed to realize that if I worked hard and focused on my goals alongside my team, I could achieve freedom. I could stand on my own two feet.

Upon graduating college, I was still unsure of what I wanted to be when I "grew up." And I did not have the luxury of spending any time unemployed or underemployed while exploring various paths. So, my initial career began as it does for many of us— through networking and asking others for input.

I reconnected with a close friend who knew my personality very well, and she suggested I investigate recruiting. She thought my "outgoing, passionate, and ambitious" personality would fare well in the field. Though I had no idea what "recruiting" was,

> *It is now my life mission to empower other women to believe in themselves despite any naysayers who may be lurking on their path to realizing their full potential – personally and professionally.*

I trusted my friend's instinct and applied for some jobs. I got an interview, went in, and fell in love with the team's comradery and the work they were getting off the ground. I was hired the next day!

The Power to Change People's Lives

During the early years of my career, I started seeing the impact I could make on people's lives. I received numerous handwritten thank you letters from candidates who I'd helped to land their dream job. They told me it would change their lives forever. I will always remember the first letter I received from a customer service representative at JP Morgan Chase. He shared with me his gratitude for assisting in his job search. He was able to now provide for his family. It would provide career growth, health benefits, and a new sense of confidence that he needed to realize his full potential. I'd never been so happy in my entire life until I started recruiting. It gave me a sense of pride, impact, and purpose that I'd never experienced before. I believed in the power to change—not only yourself, but those around you—and I began seeing how true this was when I started recruiting. Meaningful work is life-changing. Realizing I could connect people to a job that suits them (and their needs) motivated me every day.

After I mastered the art of recruiting and building relationships with candidates, I knew I was ready for my next step. But again, I was not sure what that next step should be. Should I move into recruitment operations management, human resources, or sales and marketing? During moments like this, I'd always reflect upon my childhood. I'd wish I could call my parents to ask for advice. Instead, I made a few mistakes along the way and tried out all three fields.

First, I started studying for the SPHR exam and researching how to become the best at human resources. The skills I learned during this time were really focused on technical aspects of HR and the "why" behind the people, process, and technology to support recruitment. But I quickly realized I was not passionate about payroll and the policies side of HR. I felt I would have the biggest impact and influence on driving change if I was out selling and helping clients design solutions to scale.

I then moved into a sales and marketing focused role, which brought out my creative and entrepreneurial spirit. I loved every minute of this role because it gave me the platform to drive change and influence staffing decisions across enterprise organizations at a very large scale. I spent years flying around the world visiting cities like London, Toronto, San Francisco, Hong Kong, and LA. I learned about different cultures and ways of working, and my eyes grasped the expansiveness of the world. It helped me see the impact of recruiting on a global scale. More importantly, this work and my travel gave me a sense of inner peace that I'd long been searching for, and which I suddenly realized was essential. On each airplane I boarded—and with each new, beautiful city culture I experienced—I felt a huge sense of relief and pride to be experiencing opportunities I'd been told weren't attainable as a kid.

Mental Wellness First

One major drawback to constant travel was the toll it started taking on my mental health. Focused on my work and contributing in meaningful ways to international teams, I stopped making time for myself. This led to more and more anxiety about failure and imposter syndrome. I found myself almost consistently thinking "I don't belong here" in a client meeting, or "Who wants to listen to my advice if I have five less years of experience than everyone else?" in the board room. While I was usually the youngest in the room (and often the only woman), it had never bothered me as much as it did when my fuel tank was low. Questioning myself and my abilities, I often wondered whether I should go back to school to get my MBA. I thought it would help me "be more successful." Fortunately, I had a CEO who challenged this perspective.

I will never forget the day we had a global Fortune 500 company reach out and ask us to participate in a global RFP—one of the largest I'd ever experienced. Because of the insecurities I was experiencing at that point in my career, I asked our CEO if I could hire someone with more experience to help support me. He looked at me like I had four heads. First, he asked, "Why do you need to hire someone when you already have the knowledge?" Then, he gave me the approval to bring in a consultant anyway.

After we spent a ton of money and hours working on the proposal, my CEO asked me if I felt hiring the consultant had helped. I took a step back and really thought about his question. I realized that it had helped me—but not in the way I'd originally thought. Instead, it helped me realize I'd been living with imposter syndrome and that I needed to cultivate more sustainable mental wellness. My internal dialogue always told me I could not do something because I did not have the right experience.

Right then, I shifted to focusing on my strengths and the unique and diverse experiences I brought to the team as a younger person and a woman. Again, I felt experiences from my childhood resurface as I realized these insecurities were versions of what I'd been told at a young age. Focusing on my health—mental, physical, and spiritual—has helped me keep these negative thoughts at bay when they resurface during challenging moments.

I really loved sales and marketing, but it was time to move into leadership positions. Operating as a leader, I realized I could help the fifteen individuals on my team learn and feel empowered in their work, which in turn could help many other people they serve change their lives and their clients' lives as well. While I have progressed to leading organizations of people, and I've faced my troubling narrative childhood, helping others continues to be my driving force.

Reflecting on what my father said many years ago, "the only person you can change is yourself," I finally realized this wasn't true. You can change the world around you. You can make a difference. You can influence and change people's lives. But I also realize now that helping others, and feeling a sense of belonging to that mission, is what brings all of us purpose and happiness.

It is now my life mission to empower other women to believe in themselves, despite any naysayers who may be lurking on their path, and realize their full potential—personally and professionally. I want my daughter to read this and realize that "she can." She can be anything she wants to be, go anywhere in the world, go to any school, and live with constant security, support, and love.

Kimberly Pope

Kimberly Pope is the COO of WilsonHCG and a proud mother. She graduated from Appalachian State University with a B.S. in Political Science and played on the NCAA Division I varsity field hockey team. After living in Columbus, Ohio, for a time, she met her husband and moved to Tampa, Florida, where she started at WilsonHCG.

Kim dedicates her contributions to her daughter. She wants her story to provide guidance and help to empower other women to accelerate their careers and build confidence in the workplace.

https://www.linkedin.com/in/kimpope/

PSYCHOLOGICAL RAISES

Joyce Russell

As I reflect on my career, what immediately comes to mind are all the experiences I've had during my 40 years of working. I've been fortunate to have so many amazing experiences that I even started referring to them as "psychological raises." Many of these experiences were better than money. In this chapter, I've made it my goal to explain the valuable lessons I've learned.

I believe the most important part of every organization is its people. You must have a strong and supportive organizational culture that matches up with the wants and needs of the employees. The secret to success is hiring, training, and developing the best people. You must also build an excellent culture and retain your top performers.

According to a recent Gallup study, U.S. businesses are losing a *trillion* dollars every year due to voluntary turnover. Here are some additional statistics:

- The cost of replacing an individual employee can range from one-half to two times the employee's annual salary.
- A 100-person organization with an average salary of $50,000 could have turnover and replacement costs of approximately $660,000 to $2.6 million per year.
- 52 percent of voluntarily exiting employees say their manager or organization could have done something to prevent them from leaving their job.

Turnover is expensive. You must factor in the hard and soft costs of separation, recruiting, hiring, training, lost productivity, impact on morale, and loss of knowledge—the "brain drain" that occurs when tenured, talented people leave your company.

At Adecco—where I've spent 34 years of my career—there's been a direct correlation between tenure and performance, which has led to greater profitability. The ability to hang on to talent has never been more important. So, how do we ensure that we retain talent?

First, we hire people who are a good fit; people who not only have the skills to do their job, but who also fit into our culture. Next, we create high levels of employee engagement to increase retention and decrease turnover. People want to feel special and be seen, heard, and understood. Employees stay where they are paid well, mentored, challenged, promoted, involved, appreciated, valued, empowered, and trusted. Employees want an employer who is as invested in them as they are in the company. They are looking for a relationship, not a simple transaction.

Loyalty is an emotional connection. Employees of companies with strong corporate cultures wear their company t-shirts and have a feeling of pride and loyalty for who they work for. That emotional connection is forged by helping other people grow, creating experiences, and voting with your time. Maya Angelou said, "I've learned that people will forget what you said, people will forget what you did, but people will never forget how you made them feel." Fundamentally, all of us want to feel special and appreciated. Our strongest memories (both the good and the bad) are those moments in our lives where we had a strong emotional connection to an event. That's why I strongly believe in creating superlative experiences for people. Experiences bring fun to the workplace. Fun is an underused characteristic of a company's culture, and it's the fun times that bring joy to your work and bond you to a company.

So, let's start with the definition of an experience (the noun):

Webster's Dictionary – "An event or occurrence that leaves an impression on someone."

I want to provide you with the framework that I used while creating superlative experiences over my career. I use three components to bond, ignite, and bring joy to others:

- **Listen** – Make sure you pause and listen to the people close to you. Pay attention to their stories, habits, and reactions. They'll tell you what they want if you really listen. Bring their wants, needs, delights, and goals into your experience, and you'll capture their appreciation.
- **Personalization** – Your interactions should be intentional and planned. They must be specific to people. That lets them know how important they are to you.
- **Delight** – This is truly the Cherry on Top. The small details provide the greatest impact. Adding unexpected kindness will bring so much happiness.

Necessary Surprises

We're afforded so few good surprises as adults. So, I made sure Marylou got the surprise of a lifetime during her retirement party at Disney World. Her party was planned on our final evening, following the awards ceremony at our national meeting. Everyone thought it would be a typical party with a plaque, flowers, and a speech. Of course, we did give her a plaque and flowers, and we spoke about her career. But the cherry on top came at the end when Marylou joined me on the stage.

As Marylou accepted her flowers, an incredibly beautiful Disney princess appeared from the side door on stage and started singing *When You Wish Upon a Star*. The audience—and Marylou—thought this was the surprise. Nope! The truly special moment was when the side door opened again and her two-year-old granddaughter (wearing a matching Disney princess gown) ran across the stage shouting, "Mimi! Mimi!"

See, Marylou's entire family had flown in. They walked out of that same side door to accompany her on stage and celebrate this incredible milestone with her. Marylou and her family loved the special surprise, and I'm certain our colleagues in the audience loved it just as much. They were moved to tears, and they saw how *they* would be treated after a remarkable career with Adecco. I could hardly sleep that night thinking of the happiness and joy we'd brought to Marylou, her family, and all of Adecco. It said everything about our culture and how we care for our people.

I had a similar experience as an Adecco colleague when I was selected as a torch runner for the 2000 Summer Olympic Games in Sydney, Australia. Throughout the years, Adecco has been involved with the Olympic Games. We've helped staff events around the world and have supported Olympic athletes through the U.S. Olympic and Paralympic Committee's Athlete Career and Education program. In 2000, colleagues from Adecco's United States business unit were selected to represent the company and carry the torch in the days leading up to the September 15th opening ceremony. Colleagues in other countries around the world were included as well. Adecco invited my husband, David, and my two sons, Bryson and Coleman, to make the trip with me across the world to Australia. My mom, dad, and two sisters were fortunate enough to share the experience with me as well.

Being an Olympic Games torch runner is not as easy as it looks. The torch weighs close to two pounds, and the legs of the relay range from a quarter of a mile to over five miles. Since I had been doing more Adecco work than actual *working out*, I decided I'd better train and get into shape. My training regimen included running while holding a five-pound bag of sugar over my shoulder, right beside my ear. For a month, I made regular trips to a park close to my home to run around the small fishing pond with my bag of sugar. I had to be ready to run while carrying the torch—to represent Adecco and make my family proud.

In the days leading up to our departure, I envisioned myself running through the dusty Australian Outback with kangaroos and dingoes alongside me. That was not the case, however. I was thrilled to learn I would be running in Sydney the day before the Opening Ceremony. The torch relay had begun in Olympia, Greece on May 10th, and after more than four months and 22,000 miles, the torch would be handed off to me. I would be carrying the flame that would light the cauldron in the Olympic Stadium and mark the start of the Games.

The best part of the entire experience was having my family with me. And the most memorable moment occurred as I was running down the middle of the street, between police officers on motorcycles. The sidewalks were filled with people cheering as I ran with the torch in one hand and waved with the other. Through all the adrenaline, excitement, and noise, I heard my ten-year-old son, Coleman, shouting, "That's my mother! That's my mother!" I was filled with emotion hearing him so proud of me. But at the same time, I felt guilty for having been gone so much of his life while traveling the country and growing the business. It's important to remember our children are proud of us as working parents—we are role models showcasing how their lives will be in the future as they balance work and family. Overall, it's a moment I will cherish forever.

Limitless Possibilities

Every year, we recognize and celebrate our top performers at our Superstars event. This special event is held at a different location each year. One year, we were in New Orleans and had our own Mardi Gras street parade. But my most vivid memory is of our sunrise balloon trip in Aspen, Colorado. Although everyone had to get up super early, it was such an incredible experience to see the sun rise over the mountains and then be served a champagne breakfast upon landing.

Possibilities for team events are limitless. Whether it's a nighttime tour of the monuments in Washington, D.C., a carriage ride to dinner in Charleston, South Carolina, a Cirque du Soleil show, or planting 50 pink flamingos in a front yard to celebrate an employee's birthday—it's important to create experiences and memories.

These experiences bring people together, create memories, and build lasting relationships. Strong relationships drive job satisfaction, engagement, and retention. People work for people, not companies. And people don't quit companies—they quit people. When people leave, they are quitting their direct manager. 75% of people who voluntarily quit their job are quitting their boss, according to that same Gallup analysis I mentioned before. Work relationships must be built over time and closely managed.

Build loyalty, vote with your time, manage Emotional Bank Accounts, and create exceptional experiences.

Psychological raises can also include training and development. I was fortunate to attend many outstanding training programs during my career. One of my favorites was Harvard Law School's Program on Negotiation. Those crisp fall mornings walking to class caused great waves of emotion to wash over me. I did not have the opportunity to attend Harvard as an undergraduate, but because they offered executive programs and Adecco was willing to send me, I was provided the amazing opportunity. What I ultimately learned from this experience was that my company had made an investment in me by sending me to that class in Cambridge. I learned a new set of interpersonal tools and strategies and felt more confident in negotiations. It also showed me how important I was to the company.

Over my career, I sent many colleagues to this class. I wanted them to share the same feeling and growth opportunity that I had. I looked at it as a psychological raise. It was something unexpected, yet special, that added to my experience as a colleague and deepened my sense of loyalty to my company.

Filling Our Emotional Bank Accounts With Time

One way I remain cognizant of my relationships is by using what Stephen Covey calls "The Emotional Bank Account." The Emotional Bank Account is a brilliant concept that reminds us to be aware of both our positive and negative interactions with others. Think of your Emotional Bank Account the same way you think of your checking account: your total deposits must be greater than your total withdrawals, or you will be quickly overdrawn.

Voting with your time is a major emotional deposit. We know employees feel a connection with their company when they are involved, consulted, and heard. Town hall style gatherings, monthly and quarterly all-colleague calls, FaceTime and Zoom meetings—all these tools help drive higher levels of employee communication and engagement.

Never has it been more important to keep this connection— whether it be virtually or in person. You must think creatively to keep connections alive. At the beginning of the COVID-19 pandemic in 2020, we pivoted and hosted a virtual Italian cooking class to connect with our team. We sent each team member a $50 gift card to shop at their local grocery store for the required recipe ingredients. The night of the event, the chef joined us online and taught us how to make homemade Italian lasagna and tiramisu. What joy and fun we had for the next 90 minutes! And the greatest part was that our families joined to savor these delicious dishes. This small virtual gathering had a much bigger impact than you might have expected. We hadn't seen each other in months, and this was a creative way for us to connect during such a difficult time.

I believe the best way to show people you care about them is to spend time with them. As leaders, the most precious commodity we have is time. In our personal and professional lives, we vote with our time.

In a high-level working role, you often have access to tickets, suites, upgrades, events, and opportunities that you may not otherwise have. My philosophy has always been to give them away or share them with others. The Country Music Awards (CMAs) is a great example of an experience I was able to share. I secured 25 tickets to the CMAs through a women's organization. Of course, the award show was amazing, but the best part was spending the day together getting "gussied up" to look extra special for the evening. The comradery of the entire day helped us bond and served as an emotional deposit for the team. It was one of my favorite psychological raises!

Making deposits into someone's Emotional Bank Account is easy. This could mean a simple gesture like writing a heartfelt, handwritten thank-you note; praising a colleague in front of his/her peers at a meeting; decorating a colleague's office for their birthday; telling your son/daughter that you are proud of them and why; helping a neighbor with a project; calling an old friend to catch-up; or surprising your partner with tickets to see their favorite band. The list goes on and on! I'm sure you can think of additional spectacular examples. Depositing into someone's Emotional Bank Account involves going above and beyond to put a cherry on top and letting people know how much they are valued, appreciated, and loved.

Meaningful connections between colleagues will create a vibrant culture. As a leader, when you like and respect the people you work with and show them you care, you drive employee engagement and retention. Strong bonds between colleagues at all levels of your company will elevate the performance of your employees—and in turn, your profit.

Build loyalty, vote with your time, manage Emotional Bank Accounts, and create exceptional experiences. And remember: these are all forms of psychological raises.

Citation:

McFeely & Wigert, S. M. & B.W. (2019, March 13). *This Fixable Problem Costs U.S. Businesses $1 Trillion*. Gallup. https://www.gallup.com/workplace/247391/fixable-problem-costs-businesses-trillion.aspx

Joyce Russell

As President of the Adecco Group U.S. Foundation, Joyce is committed to making the future work for everyone. The Foundation launched in January of 2019 with a focus on up-/reskilling American workers and helping to ensure work equality for all.

In 1987, Joyce joined Adecco USA, Inc. (Adecco) as a Branch Manager in Charlotte, North Carolina. From 2004-2018, she served as the President of Adecco and led the largest business unit of Adecco Group North America with over 450 branch locations, approximately 1,600 colleagues, and a diverse portfolio of clients.

During her time at Adecco, Joyce has firmly established her passion for working with people and providing new opportunities for employees and companies alike. She constantly strives for growth—both personally and professionally—while remaining focused on work-related programs, partnerships, and investments that create greater economic opportunity for American workers.

Joyce is a board member of Celsius Holdings, Inc. and serves as Chair of the Compensation Committee. For the 2020-2021 term, she served as Chairman of the Board of Directors of the American Staffing Association. Additionally, Joyce is a board member of Dress for Success Worldwide, a founding member of Paradigm for Parity, a member of C200, International Women's Forum, Women Corporate Directors, and is a panelist and participant at the World Economic Forum in Davos and Fortune's Most Powerful Women Summits. Joyce holds a Bachelor of Arts degree in business and communications from Baylor University.

https://www.linkedin.com/in/joycerusselladecco/

BE THE CHANGE

Leslie M. Vickrey

"Let nothing dim the light that shines from within."
– Maya Angelou

An Introduction

Hello!

My name is Leslie Vickrey. I'm a mother, wife, daughter, sister, aunt, friend, and entrepreneur. I'm a person with imperfections like everyone else. My story isn't necessarily unique, but my hope is that you'll walk away with at least one idea you can share with someone or put into action in your professional career and/or personal life.

My story began like this: I was 21, had recently graduated college, and was pulling out of my driveway in Saginaw, Michigan, in a Pontiac T1000 with around $300 in travelers checks (yes, travelers checks!) and a credit card with a $500 limit (which I thought was a ton of money). I was headed to Colorado, with all of my belongings in the hatch of my car. During the 20-hour drive, I belted out every Fleetwood Mac lyric I knew with a full heart and screeching lungs. I was completely free. In my mind, I had made it.

On my way to the small town of Vail, Colorado, for a broadcasting gig, my car broke down. I didn't have enough money to make it there, so I slept on my friend's couch in Denver and waited tables until I could get back on my feet. I had no idea that moment would be the beginning of a pivotal chapter in my life: the start of my adult, personal, and professional journey. In the ensuing years, I'd go from professional ski-bum to small-town waitress, from an intern at McDonald's to working public relations at Junior Achievement, to running global marketing for Spherion's technology division, and finally, to owning and leading my own company. What a journey it's been!

Surrounded By Strong Women

Before we talk about my entrepreneurial journey, you should know where I came from. Born in the early '70s in Flint, Michigan, I was raised with a Midwestern grit that would ultimately carry me through many of life's twists and turns.

The women in my family played such a profound role in my life, but I didn't really think too much about that until I was deep into my professional journey. When I look back at the lives of my grandmothers, I see an interesting contrast between two women. One was a successful entrepreneur. She owned several children's clothing stores across Detroit during a time when most women didn't work. My other grandmother—a budding singer who turned down an on-air singing job—was told that her role was to stay home and raise their family. My own mother went back to finish college in her 30s, then went on to become CEO of multiple credit unions. Saying I was raised by strong women would be an understatement.

My parents divorced when I was very young. I can't even recall meeting another family with divorced parents until middle school. My grandmother, the entrepreneur, was also divorced. I followed suit by getting divorced. I even had a business partnership end poorly, which my attorney referred to as a divorce. I knew what was happening: I wasn't trusting my own gut, and I was making decisions that weren't great for me. I didn't fully trust myself, and I didn't have the confidence to do what was best for me.

One might ask, "How could you struggle with confidence when you were raised by such powerful women?" Well, it simply wasn't that easy. My confidence issues started at a young age, when I was still who I now think of as "Little Leslie."

From Little Leslie to CEO

I believe I was born confident. I have no reason to believe otherwise.

But when other people started teasing me at an early age (from what I've now realized was just their own insecurities), I let it get the best of me. In a split second, my confidence was stripped away. I've since learned that this doesn't just happen in childhood—some people continue to push other people down their entire lives. I'm not sure why.

Tip: *One of the best gifts you can give your children, especially girls, is that of confidence. It will last a lifetime.*

I'm part Lebanese, part Italian. I had more facial and leg hair than the average girl. (Okay, here's the truth: I had a full-on mustache in elementary school and begged my mom to let me shave my legs). Kids called me Ralph Macchio and the Karate Kid. Even later in life, I was told that I looked like Cat Stevens (it must have been the dark, slightly out of control, curly hair). I was told I wasn't pretty enough. I also developed earlier than most girls, so teasing ensued. Kids were ruthless. I didn't have the confidence at that point to really use my voice.

All that was coupled with a nickname I was given, Lazy Leslie. While it got to me as a child, reflecting on it as an adult, I do believe it pushed me to be a stronger person.

One day, I had what I can only describe as a profound, life-changing experience. Someone asked me if I had ever envisioned myself as a little girl. I never had. I'd never closed my eyes and pictured Little

Leslie. But when I did for the first time, I saw this cute little girl in pigtails with an incredible life ahead of her. She was pre-Ralph Macchio, at the beginning of where my struggles with confidence started. Another session of envisioning this allowed me to let Little Leslie know I always had her back. I knew she was protected, and it was OK for her to go.

By the way, this envisioning exercise occurred at a place I have been to on separate occasions with my best friends, my mom, and with my company before COVID. It's called Miraval. It was my version of self-help, and it allowed me to heal by fully opening my eyes and heart. It helped me trust myself and give myself to others in a more complete way.

I often say I went through my 20s with my eyes closed. They opened in my 30s. I see this often in other people, too. My hope for everyone is that no matter your age, you can open your eyes and see what's right in front of you. You can live your life to the fullest.

Living life to the fullest was a piece of advice I got from my grandmother (the singer). She always told me to keep doing what I was doing (as an independent woman, with my own money, running my own company) and to live my life the way I wanted. Those simple words (live your life) are always in my head. When I make decisions others think are risky, her advice is at the forefront of my mind.

Never Underestimate the Power of Your Network

My path to CEO started in high school. I discovered my love and passion for writing when I was assigned to write a story about someone in my English class. This person was often bullied, and I loved being able to tell his story. After publishing, it was a joy seeing the changed perception people had of him. I'd accomplished that by being able to share who he really was and how he'd impacted my life. That's when I knew writing was for me.

I studied journalism at Central Michigan University, graduated, then landed a broadcast journalist internship in Vail. As I was leaving my house in Michigan to start my journey to Colorado, my neighbor ran out and told me that a friend of ours from high school lived in Denver. He gave me her phone number. I wouldn't realize the impact of his gesture until a little later, but it would significantly change my life.

We didn't have cell phones when I was driving to Vail. Naturally, my T1000 broke down. So, I crossed the highway, went to a nearby restaurant, and called my high school friend who lived in Denver. She took me in, and I slept on her couch until I'd saved up enough money to get a futon. She got me a job waiting tables, which was one of the best times of my life. I became more confident and independent. It set me up for the next stage of my life. You'll notice a common thread throughout my journey: the power of connections and creating your network.

First: If you don't ask, you'll never be told yes. And second: Remember to build, cultivate, and leverage your network.

With my parents encouraging me to get a job related to my degree, and with the help of a personal connection, I landed my first "real" job as an internal communication specialist at McDonald's Corporation. Before I knew it, I was off to Chicago. They also had a broadcast network for their franchise locations, and when I went through training, they told me my voice, hair, and clothes were all wrong. Right then, I realized it wasn't the broadcasting part that was so important to me—it was the writing element.

At 23, I was given an opportunity to support the Global CEO of McDonald's with a special project. I would be the company representative, and I'd help plan a Junior Achievement Hall of Fame event. I'd gained exposure to the McDonald's C-Suite at such a young age, and I didn't want to take the opportunity for granted.

I was making $10 an hour. I could barely afford to pay highway tolls. Knowing what a big opportunity it was, my grandma (the singer) helped me buy a nice dress for the event. Then, during the event, something remarkable happened. The head of McDonald's marketing, Jack Daly, told me, "Leslie, that's going to be you up on stage one day." I politely thanked him, but internally I was thinking: "You must be crazy!" I didn't see in myself what Jack saw in me.

If You Don't Ask, You'll Never Hear "Yes"

After about a year, I decided the job wasn't for me. I wanted to return to Colorado. (As you can imagine, my parents were disappointed. The McDonald's job had been a truly wonderful opportunity.) My heart was in the mountains, and living somewhere I loved was crucial to me.

Turning to my network again, I reached out to my Junior Achievement contact in Chicago to see if they had any openings in Denver. Sure enough, they did. I ended up running events and public relations for Junior Achievement, and I attribute my success to having a strong network (of course, I was also very good at my job). Women are known for sacrificing their networks when rising in companies and/or starting a family. So, I'd like to mention two vital lessons here. First: If you don't ask, you'll never be told yes. And second: Remember to build, cultivate, and leverage your network.

Fast forward to 1998. I moved to Chicago for a marketing role in a global, publicly traded company. I ended up gaining a ton of experience there, exposure to global markets, M&A integration, and much more.

After a few years, I was faced with a situation where the company was moving its headquarters to Atlanta. I stayed in Chicago and found a new job, but the company I went to was investing in marketing for the first time and, unfortunately, I realized they weren't a good fit. I eventually had a *Eureka!* moment as an entrepreneur. I was going to start my own company: ClearEdge Marketing.

I didn't have a business plan when I started ClearEdge. I didn't have funding, either. I didn't have a lot of personal responsibilities, which was helpful. I *did* have clients right out of the gate, thanks to my former boss and other work colleagues. So again, by leveraging my network and connections, I was fortunate enough to get started. I had a strong network of people who supported me and helped with my growth. Starting ClearEdge was no small task, but I knew it was worth the risk.

If You See It, You Can Be It

As I was presenting to a classroom of business school students at DePaul University, one of the students asked me if I'd always wanted to be an entrepreneur. I thought, "No, I always wanted to be a writer. I wanted to be a journalist, that's what I always wanted to be." But there I stood, an entrepreneur. I'd always worked for other people, but one day an idea had come to me, and I'd gone for it. I'd believed in myself and taken another leap of faith. It was like when I had traveled out West—only this time I was a little wiser in my approach.

At that moment, I realized why it hadn't been such a big deal to start a company. I grew up in a family of entrepreneurs. If I could see it, I could be it.

If You Hear Something, Say Something

I struggled with imposter syndrome early on as a CEO. It was like childhood all over again. People were content to strip away my confidence. They'd say small things that would chip away at me, like: "You have your own company? That's so *cute!*" Or another of my favorites: "You don't really seem like a CEO. I mean, once you start talking, I get it, you're a CEO."

In both cases, I'd heard something, but failed to respond. These were perfect opportunities to use my voice. But in the moment, I was rendered speechless. So, let this be a lesson. It's critical to find and use your voice, whether for yourself or someone else.

That's a lesson I learned from Robin Mee—also featured in this book—when she used her voice on my behalf in an uncomfortable situation. She stood up for me and had my back. From that moment on, I knew I had to carry the torch forward for myself *and* for others.

For the first time in my career, I was being recognized for my achievements. I'm used to helping clients get recognized or recognizing people on our team, not the other way around. People say women never take the time to slow down and celebrate their accomplishments. I am certainly one of those women.

I won a few industry awards, made "Who's Who in Tech" lists, got inducted into the UIC Entrepreneurial Hall of Fame, and was named one of Enterprising Women Magazine's Women of the Year. I was sitting on boards for Chicago Innovation and i.c.stars. I was frequently speaking at events. But still, I didn't see in myself what others saw in me. I even questioned one of the awards—I thought it was a pay-to-play opportunity. But then I found out it was extremely legit and that several people had nominated me!

I even started a company called ARA—which stands for Attract, Retain, and Advance women in technology—with two of my best friends, Megan McCann and Jane Hamner. The topic of confidence comes up in every single talk we give. One survey we administered even returned the following results: One piece of advice men have for women and women have for women is to be more confident.

My dad always said, "You have to look in the mirror and love yourself first." So again, why do so many people struggle with this when we aren't born not loving ourselves? And why do we let outside influences bring us down? The best gift our parents and those around children can give is to instill confidence. Get kids to focus on living their best lives and to come as they are, instead of why they aren't a certain way (skinny, pretty, smart, social—the list goes on and on).

Then, July of 2015 came along. I spent my entire ClearEdge life building a company with a flexible model and work environment. We have over 55 people on our team, and we service clients around the world. I don't care where people work. It doesn't matter to me. We had a virtual model from day one. We focused on talent, not location. Talent, accountability, giving people a chance to have a career AND raise a family AND take care of their parents AND care for special needs kids AND travel the world—those are the things that matter to me. But I never realized how much that model would change my life in the long run.

I also have a husband who supports me 100% (I cannot stress this enough, a strong support network is key to being successful in all things life). He isn't intimidated by my success whatsoever, and he's supportive of my passions and purpose. That's incredibly important to me, especially after having failed at marriage in the past. I allowed myself to build trust and open up, and I found someone who loved me for me.

After seven years of marriage, and at the age of 42, we found out we were pregnant. We never thought it was in the cards for us. I was petrified. People questioned me left and right—and notice how I said questioned, not encouraged. Sure, plenty of people were supportive. But when you are already struggling with confidence, you tend to focus on the little things people say.

One day, for example, I sat down with a mentor and shared that I was pregnant. His response was: "Oh, what's going to happen to your company now? You're going to close, right?" In that moment, I had a choice to make. I could get defensive, get upset, say nothing, or turn it around and say something. I finally felt confident to use my voice and said: "You own your company, how did you do it? How did you raise your daughter and run the company? Perhaps you can help mentor and teach me." It was a see it, say it moment that worked for me.

Another time, I went into a sales call where we were pitching a brand strategy. I was wearing a vest, so you couldn't tell I was pregnant. At the end of the meeting, they verbally told us we'd won the deal. But as soon as they heard I was pregnant, they started panicking. They questioned how we would deliver the project while I was on leave. I thought to myself: "Really? I can't believe that in this day and age I'm about to lose a deal because I'm pregnant." We ended up winning the deal, but it was another opportunity to politely see something and say something.

Defeat Your Inner "Evil DJ"

What I realized was that, all this time, I'd been a victim of a phrase my sister Vicky shared with me, the "Evil DJ," which is playing the same negative song over and over in your head. What if I speak up at a meeting and it's a terrible idea? What if I say the wrong thing? I had to turn off the "Evil DJ" asking those questions. Occasionally, I still hear it. But now I'm strong enough to shut it down. I know having negative thoughts is something a lot of people struggle with—it's important to know you're not alone.

Along the way, I realized that—even with all the awards and recognition—my biggest challenges AND accomplishments were still ahead of me. I was going to be a mom. My flexible work model, the one I fought to make functional for everyone else BUT me, would now actually work FOR me. My team stepped up, forced me to take time off, and told me they wanted more responsibility. I slowly started stepping away from day-to-day work. I had to start acting like a CEO. A CEO who was also a wife, mom, and who was driven by her career.

We had our son, Greyson, and immediately people started asking if I was disappointed we'd had a boy because of all I do to support women. So, one day, I brought Greyson into a women's luncheon, an event our company has sponsored as part of TechServe Alliance's annual conference for the past 15 years. My dad brought Greyson to me as I stood in front of the room. I wanted to share the idea of allyship, prove the point that I was thrilled to have a boy because he would be raised in a diverse family, one where his mom is a CEO at work and where we are co-CEOs as parents at home. Greyson would be part of the next generation of change. His ability to see equality firsthand, I felt, was a gift that would ultimately become a critical part of change.

Full Circle

My husband and I had bought a second home in Breckenridge back when we thought kids weren't in the picture. He worked ski patrol in Keystone back in the day, and you'll recall that I loved Colorado. My heart was in the mountains.

My friend who'd helped me when I had $300 to my name was the same person who represented us when we bought that home. The years between were incredible. Sometimes, I feel like I've already lived three lives. Coming out on this end of the road, I'm able to see so much more clearly that my passion and purpose were closely aligned.

Be A Light That Shines for Other Women

Why is my advice so important? Well, I feel this overwhelming need to help the next generation rise up. I want to lift them up and ensure they don't experience the same uncomfortable situations and unfair business practices I experienced. I will forever follow my mantra of raising up those around me and setting up the next generation for a better life, just like my grandmothers, my mom, my stepmother Kathie, and so many other women did for me. Will you join me? Let's be the change together.

Leslie M. Vickrey

Leslie Vickrey is a marketing expert and business advisor. She began her career with McDonald's Corporation and found a niche in technology and talent as the head of marketing for Spherion's technology division. She founded ClearEdge Marketing in 2006, a full-service marketing agency for talent and technology firms.

Leslie's impact in the HR, tech, and marketing communities far exceeds her day-to-day work as CEO. Passionate about the importance of diversity, Leslie is a frequent speaker on the topic and even co-founded ARA, an organization that has impacted over 6,000 people and seeks to Attract, Retain, and Advance women in technology.

Active in the communities she serves, Leslie is part of the Women Business Collaborative Staffing Leadership Council. She's a member of the American Staffing Association's Women in Leadership Council, is on the Board of Advisors for Chicago Innovation, and was recognized as one of Chicago's 100 Most Compelling Innovators and Entrepreneurs. She's part of the UIC Entrepreneurship Hall of Fame, was named as a Staffing Industry Analysts Top 50 DEI Influencer, and was named one of the Enterprising Women of the Year.

Leslie is a contributor to industry publications such as Recruiting Daily and Entrepreneur. She's a frequent industry speaker and the host of TheEdge, a podcast that focuses on executive women in recruitment.

Leslie resides in Colorado with her husband, Collin, and son, Greyson.

https://www.linkedin.com/in/lvickrey/
lvickrey@clearedgemarketing.com

GET COMFORTABLE BEING UNCOMFORTABLE – WOMEN BREAKING THROUGH TO MANAGEMENT AND EXECUTIVE ROLES IN THE STAFFING INDUSTRY

Ursula Williams

"How did you get into the staffing industry?"
"What was your career path like along the way?"
"What advice do you have for the future women leaders of the staffing industry?"

Those are the three most common career-related questions I receive today. My top-of-mind responses are filled with enthusiasm, passion, joy, and encouragement. How could they not be? I've had a blessed career. I've held every internal staffing industry role in field operations, worked with extremely gifted people, and solved workforce talent issues for Fortune 500 companies while helping people find great jobs. Always open to new experiences and challenges, I've traveled across the country opening offices and expanding brands through company and franchise operations. I built and ran corporate departments in marketing, operations, training, and even information technology. By 30, I was an area Vice President—a position I achieved a few years sooner than expected.

Throughout the years, I've worked with some of the most brilliant minds in the business and strategists from the world's leading consultancy firms. Together we solved complex strategy, organizational design, and rebrand issues for what is today the largest staffing firm in the world. My work has brought me all over the world, including to Amsterdam, Berlin, Cape Town, Lisbon, London, Montreal, Prague, Rome, Singapore, and more. Promotions came fast (10 in 20 years), and new challenges came faster. I was the person family and friends referred to as the happiest working person they knew, and it was true. It was all exhilarating to me—my work, the rollercoaster of ups and downs in the business, the personal achievements and financial rewards. Making a difference in people's lives, having fun, and making money were the ideals I lived by.

> *I was the person family and friends referred to as the happiest working person they knew, and it was true.*

Friendships and bonds forged in staffing are amongst the strongest one can imagine. Maybe it's the work, maybe it's the industry , maybe it's because relationships matter so much in the business. Likely it's all the above. Some of my longest relationships are with people I worked with in staffing for over 25 years. Ironically, most of them are men. A lot of the women I started with either chose to remain as individual contributors or opted out of the staffing industry in pursuit of more predictable, controllable work. Fast forward to where I am today: Chief Operating Officer at Staffing Industry Analysts. Nowadays, a major topic discussion (backed by research) is the lack of women occupying executive leadership roles in the staffing industry.

This is a major issue that has bothered me throughout my career and still does today. Why do women comprise a large majority of internal staff at staffing firms yet are generally underrepresented at the executive and board levels across the staffing industry?

What was it that set me on the course to where I am today? What advice could I give to women pursuing leadership positions in the staffing industry that would encourage them to stay the course and break through?

In pursuit of answers, I reflected on major milestones in my career. This chapter is a summation of some of the lessons I've learned along the way. And while women may not occupy as many executive level jobs in staffing (or in general) as they should, it's never too late to shift the tide.

Embrace Change

Like many who work in staffing, the industry found me. During my senior year in college, I applied and was accepted for a paid internship at Apple. The envy of my classmates and the star in my professor's eyes, I proudly reported to Apple HQ a few weeks after graduation, complete with an Apple sticker on the windshield of my new (commuter) car. Within an hour of arriving, things started to fall apart. I learned that I was what they called a "payroll employee," which meant I was not an employee of Apple, but rather an employee of a company called Adia (now Adecco), a temporary agency. How would I explain that to my family and friends? What did it mean? Clearly there was a mistake. One of the greatest achievements of my young adult life was turning out to be one of the most uncomfortable professional moments I'd ever experienced. And as the days passed, the situation worsened. The paid internship position I was recruited for was no longer being sponsored. I was going to be unemployed, in a matter of days!

That terrible employment experience ended up being monumental for me. It was the catalyst to my entry into staffing. Upon hearing I no longer worked at Apple, Adia recruited me to work as a recruiter in their award-winning Palo Alto office, which was filled with high performers who quickly became my greatest mentors, supporters, sponsors, and friends. Becoming a Staffing Manager at Adia was a blessing, but it was also way out of my comfort zone. I didn't know anything about recruiting, employment, managing people, or labor laws. The training was outstanding, and the expectations were extremely high. Being an overachiever, I was motivated by loftier goals. Every day was more exciting than the previous day. I couldn't wait to start making placements, which was an expectation during week three. Thanks to my tenured colleagues in the office and my ability to remember people and details regarding their skills, I was able to connect people with jobs and achieve my goals.

The pace was fast. So fast that mistakes could be made. My greatest mistake came around week four on the job. I placed a forklift driver—a proven performer, someone who previously worked for us and did a great job—at a major account. It was a terrific placement, my best match yet. All was going well. That is, until day three on the job, when my proven performer accidentally placed the forks of his forklift through a wall at the client's warehouse. This wall separated the client's warehouse from the office of the client's CEO. Not good! There were no injuries, and the damage was not extensive, but the accident did not go over well. To make matters worse, I overlooked a major background detail in my haste to fill the job: The forklift operator's forklift license was expired! While my manager and colleagues were very supportive, the mistake was highly transparent and terribly uncomfortable for me. So uncomfortable that I contemplated if I'd chosen the right career path.

Nonetheless, I stayed with it. And thanks to a great group of people around me, I quickly mastered the role and continued to love it. I even won an award for excellence in my first year.

Be Confident

After a couple years of working as a recruiter, a marketing position opened in Adia's Corporate Headquarters. Marketing was my obsession. I had majored in business with an emphasis in marketing, I read books constantly about marketing, and I attended conferences and seminars on marketing. A role in marketing, with a company I loved, was a dream come true. As luck would have it, I met the VP of Marketing for Adia during a recognition event a few months prior and expressed my interest in marketing. I was told the position was mine if I wanted it. It was a perfect promotion for the next step in my career, but when the call from the internal recruiter came, I hesitated. The notion of telling my manager and my co-workers—people who had taken a risk on me, invested hours training and developing me—that I was leaving them for a job at corporate was going to be extremely uncomfortable. Thankfully, I took the job. And true to form, my manager and co-workers were extremely happy and beyond proud for my promotion.

Working at Adia Corporate in Marketing was a highlight of my entire staffing career. Having knowledge of the business proved to be extremely beneficial at corporate, and having relationships and contacts in the field operations was a key to my success. Ideas to support the branches and build the brand flowed easily. I learned so much about the entire department and other departments that I became instrumental in building bridges between departments and field operations. That resulted in two promotions *and* the pinnacle of all corporate awards—Adia Employee of the Year—all within three years. The Employee of the Year award came with two tickets to anywhere in the US, an all-expense paid trip for two, plus spending cash. The winner also was rewarded a large bronze plaque with the image of their face on it, which hung in our executive wing alongside previous winners. This was a BIG honor; I was beyond appreciative, and I planned to work at Adia for the rest of my life.

The following year, drastic changes occurred at my dream job and company. Senior management shifted and new management came in. People I admired were leaving the company. Getting work done and performing at the level I was accustomed to became difficult because sign offs took longer, budgets were in question, and projects were stalling. Recruiters (from competitors to Adia) were calling with opportunities for larger and higher paying roles, but I felt loyal and committed to the company that had taken a risk on me and taught me everything I knew. My face was hanging on a plaque in the executive wing—I couldn't go to a competitor!

Suddenly, everything changed overnight, and I knew the next several weeks were going to be extremely uncomfortable. While at a retirement dinner for a senior member of the Marketing department, I happened to be seated next to one of the most dynamic women I had ever met: Dianne Borsini Burr. She was not with Adia at the time, but she was the person who opened the first Adia office in the US. She had recently opened her own staffing company focused on Finance and Accounting. While I knew nothing about finance and accounting staffing, or her company's vision, financial status, and growth plans, I knew that I had to work for her!

Lucky for me, Dianne felt the same way. Within a week, I had an offer too good to resist. Resigning was an incredibly difficult thing to do. Once again, I had that uncomfortable feeling I got every time I was faced with a major personal change. Adia presented me with a generous counteroffer that included working in Switzerland on a special assignment for a year. While the offer was incredibly tempting, the recruiter in me knew better than to accept a counteroffer. To ease my guilt, I gave Adia a three-week notice (two was customary). Within a short amount of time, I was gainfully employed as a Marketing Manager in a small regional finance and accounting staffing firm. I made nearly double the money, had a five-minute commute, was on the executive team, and reported directly to Dianne, the Founder and CEO.

The first few months were terrifying and thrilling at the same time. Nothing had really prepared me for working at a corporate headquarters for a start-up! Every dollar spent, every decision I made, every minute of my time directly impacted the company and my dynamic new boss. Priorities opened and closed fast. The standard of excellence was high, and speed was paramount. There was no time to overanalyze projects. Time was money. Twelve-hour days (often longer) were common, but they went by quickly. People, including myself, had to be pushed out the door and reminded to go home. Energy was high, laughter was contagious, food and drink (sodas and water) were abundant, and the recognition and celebrations were frequent and extremely memorable.

Within six months, I was promoted from a Marketing Manager to a Director of Marketing and Operations. Once again, I was pushed out of my comfort zone, grasping at learning the operations of an extremely successful startup company. Having the best teacher in the world (Dianne) made learning the operations more manageable.

Recognize Your Worth the Way Your Mentors Do

The next year went by lightning-fast. Everything was going great. We were working hard, growing the company, making money, and having a lot of fun. I had tons to learn but was finally getting comfortable at the company and in my role. Then, suddenly, it all changed.

Dianne called me into her office to have a *career discussion*. She knew my goal was to be VP of Marketing of our larger organization, even if it meant giving up Operations. That promotion was at least two years away, so the timing of our meeting was suspect. But then it all became clear. During that meeting, I was presented with an opportunity that put me at a major career crossroads. She explained that to become a VP of Marketing (at this organization), a prerequisite was to run a large field operation for at least three years. The San Francisco Area Vice President role was *coincidentally* open, and she wanted me to take it. My head started to spin, my stomach ached, and I nearly passed out. Running the San Francisco Area operation was way out of my scope and capability for a variety of reasons, the first being my lack of experience. How could this be happening? How could she think I would succeed at that job? What if I failed? How could a failed Area Vice President ever get promoted to Vice President of Marketing? What if I said no?

Seeing the fear in my eyes, Dianne started laughing. Then, as if she was a mind reader, she proceeded to tell me everything I was feeling and thinking. She knew I was terrified, afraid of failing and risking my reputation and dream role. She also knew that in a very short period I'd learned a lot and was excelling in my current role. She knew I was finally comfortable and didn't want to be made uncomfortable yet again.

There was a tremendous amount of pressure working in field operations. In this organization, it was the equivalent of running an entire business. It came with full profit and loss responsibility, hiring, training, retaining of the team, and running all divisions (direct-hire, temporary, temporary-to-direct hire) and all functions (sales, recruitment, administration). I also was tasked with developing and executing the business strategy and plan for the market. The hours were long, and the schedule was extremely unpredictable. In addition to all this, the San Francisco Area—the company's flagship office—wasn't doing well at the time. It needed a lot of work, particularly a seasoned staffing executive at the helm. But to achieve my next career goal, this uncomfortable step was a must.

As she continued to talk, the daunting thought of leaving the staffing industry started to creep into my mind. Perhaps this industry was not for me. Maybe the pace in which we worked wasn't sustainable. I was 29, a married homeowner looking to start a family. Perhaps it was time to settle down into a more manageable role. I wouldn't be the first woman in staffing to opt out of the business due to the intense demands on relationships and family. Several co-workers my age had chosen to decline management roles and remain as individual contributors or move to more support-level roles. Others pursued management roles in more predictable businesses. Perhaps it was my time to exit the staffing industry.

Thankfully, Dianne was extremely persuasive and determined. It was clear she'd be my greatest supporter, teacher, and mentor, and that she'd ensure I had what was necessary to succeed in my new role. With trepidation, I accepted the promotion. And while that first year was filled with a lot of new beginnings and lessons learned, it was also one of the most fulfilling years (and experiences) of my entire career. Working directly in the business brought me back to the earlier days when I was a recruiter. Leading a team of incredible staffing professionals (rookies and senior leaders) who were dedicated to finding people jobs and helping managers find great employees was intoxicating. Within our first year, we won the annual award for Most Improved Branch. And within a couple of years, we won an annual award for Branch of the Year, which came with a Leader of the Year award as well. I still valued working with great people, having fun, and making money.

Overcoming Challenges Leads to Achievement

While on maternity leave (yes, I started that family!) nearly three years from the day I accepted the Area Vice President role in San Francisco, I was promoted to VP of Marketing (followed by several large executive promotions over the next 12 years). I became the senior leader of the group and went on to oversee exhilarating growth, expansion, acquisitions, and international business. I ultimately became an executive in what is today's largest international staffing company in the world, followed by joining the only other company I ever wanted to work for: Staffing Industry Analysts. My executive leadership experiences are a thrilling journey I'll share in our next book!

What was it about me that made me push through the difficult times in my career? Those times where so many women I admired opted to leave the industry? What was it about the people who recruited me into the staffing industry, the women who invested relentless hours teaching me the business, supporting me, sponsoring me, and believing in me?

One thing they all had in common was that they were *comfortable being uncomfortable*. They had the confidence to push through the difficult moments, knowing those moments were a small part of the journey to success. They took risks and were not afraid of being exposed or of having temporary setbacks.

I've experienced many peaks and valleys in my career, and I've learned to embrace and enjoy both. I've learned to become comfortable being uncomfortable. In fact, I've mastered it. The staffing industry is a cyclical business that is extremely economically sensitive. It's an emotional business dependent on relationships. People come and go, which can be hard to adjust to. It's a highly fragmented business, where acquisitions and mergers occur and can be extremely disruptive. And as we've recently learned, every so often a pandemic comes around and disrupts everything. By learning to be *comfortable being uncomfortable*, and by being confident taking risks, your challenges will become opportunities and you'll become a stronger and more qualified leader. You'll take control of the difficult moments in your career and learn to enjoy them as much as the best times! After all, it's all just *temporary*.

Ursula Williams

Ursula Williams was appointed Chief Operating Officer (COO) of Staffing Industry Analysts in 2019. As COO, Williams is responsible for overseeing all of SIA's commercial offerings, corporate functions of marketing, memberships, communications, technology operations, and driving innovation and integration in the company's leading platforms and offerings.

Prior to her appointment as COO, Williams served as EVP at SIA. There, she bridged various SIA departments, resulting in superior and innovative products and services for the staffing and workforce solutions ecosystem. While occupying this role, Williams led the company in developing SIA's newest and award-winning conference, Collaboration in the Gig Economy. She also assisted in a rebrand to reflect SIA's global growth and ongoing role in providing business intelligence, research, and frontline insights across an increasingly dynamic and complex talent landscape.

Williams joined SIA in 2015 as SVP of Global Strategy and Marketing. She has over 25 years of industry leadership experience. Before becoming part of the SIA team, Williams held senior executive positions at Randstad Professionals and Vedior/Select Appointments, where she oversaw strategy, sales, and delivery for the largest contingent labor buyers in the division. She has also been responsible for field and corporate level operations, new product development, branding, web strategies, sales/client development, and talent recruitment programs.

Williams was recently appointed as a Council Member to the newly-formed Staffing Leadership Council in the U.S., which is part of the Women's Business Collaborative (WBC). The Council is committed to the acceleration of an equitable and inclusive workplace environment in the Staffing Industry.

https://www.linkedin.com/in/ursula-williams-b79a54/

CPSIA information can be obtained
at www.ICGtesting.com
Printed in the USA
BVHW072242260522
638165BV00004B/22

9 781956 914337